The Moment

The Moment

By Legendary Celebrity Psychic Kenny Kingston

as told to Valerie Porter

BearManor Media
2011

The Moment: By Legendary Celebrity Psychic Kenny Kingston
as told to Valerie Porter

© 2011 Kenny Kingston & Valerie Porter

All rights reserved.

For information, address:

BearManor Media
P. O. Box 71426
Albany, GA 31708

bearmanormedia.com

Typesetting and layout by John Teehan

Published in the USA by BearManor Media

ISBN— 1-59393-629-X
978-1-59393-629-7

Table of Contents

Introduction 1

Chapter 1   What is a moment? 5

Chapter 2   Don't wait for life to happen to you 19

Chapter 3   What a difference a day made 33

Chapter 4   Stop fearing and start living 53

Chapter 5   Learn from the past; live in the future 67

Chapter 6   Success 79

Chapter 7   I love life 89

Chapter 8   Our personal moments 97

Index 105

To everyone who helped us achieve our moments…

And to all who are about to realize their own moment.

Introduction

Just Once in a Lifetime
A man knows a moment
One wonderful moment
When Fate takes his hand…
— Singer/songwriter Anthony Newley

Think about the moment that changed your life—defined your life—shaped your destiny. It may have been good or bad; either way it was no doubt very powerful. It left an imprint on your mind or heart and made you realize that life would never again be quite the same.

For some, it is the moment they fell in love. For others, their moment is when they finally felt successful. Some people recall their moment as the time when they felt the strongest. Still others recognize their moment as the time when they felt they'd realized their true purpose in life.

A dear friend of mine was the multi-talented singer/actor/songwriter Anthony Newley. He, with his partner Leslie Bricusse, was responsible for many wonderful songs, including "Candy Man," "What Kind of Fool am I?" and "Who Can I Turn To?" But perhaps my favorite of Tony's songs was "Once in a Lifetime." As I began assembling notes for this book, the lyrics to that song came hauntingly to mind. They represent the essence of what I will be addressing as you and I journey through the following pages.

It seemed appropriate to begin this book with some of the song's lyrics, because they speak of knowing *one wonderful moment, when fate takes our hand.*

I have long believed that every moment of life is precious and each experience is an opportunity for learning and for the betterment of our soul. But I have also come to understand that in the midst of the many phases of our lives there is one particularly powerful moment when fate does indeed take our hand. The key is to recognize that moment when it comes along, to make the most of such a moment and of course to be grateful for it.

In my long career I have been spiritual counselor and friend to people from all walks of life. Your enjoyment of this book will not depend upon your belief in the psychic world, though today it has become increasingly more popular to believe. But even if you only have a healthy curiosity about the spirit world I trust you will find this book of interest since it is primarily intended to provide inspiration and motivation.

Yet having said that you do not need to be a firm believer in the psychic world, I must say that I am perhaps best known for having given psychic readings and messages to famous personalities of yesterday and today. Over the course of my private consultations I have been privy to the highs and lows of these clients and friends and I have been told of their pivotal moments in life, when they knew their life had changed.

At first I thought it was just a coincidence that many of these successful and notable people had had an experience that they felt changed their life. But after hearing time and again the wonder and the gratitude in their voices as they shared their moment with me, and after hearing similar stories from people in all walks of life, I came to the conclusion that it is something we are all destined to experience. And I realized that perhaps the greatest joy comes in the exploration and discovery of that moment.

I have asked a few celebrity friends to share their moments with you. That is not to say that this will be strictly a celebrity-oriented book or only about the famous. But if you are anything like me I am sure you will agree that being able to put a face and name to an idea can often help to better express that idea. My hope is that because you will be familiar with some of the personalities sprinkled throughout these pages you will be able to respond to and identify with them. And of course most importantly, I hope that you thoroughly enjoy their stories.

In most of the cases where celebrity comments or stories are included, I will wager that you will be surprised by what they chose as their moment. One hint is to expect the unexpected. Be prepared to be amused, touched and enlightened by their life experiences. And you may find that you have had a similar experience in your own life.

That brings me to the book's main focus: YOU. I want you to begin thinking about your own life. Sometimes just the pleasure of taking time to look back at events and people from our past can be an inspirational process. We may find that something we thought was a painful experience was really a stepping stone to a brighter future. Perhaps someone who seemed insignificant in our life can, in retrospect, be seen as an energizing and necessary force of influence.

In addition to the private consultations that I have given, I have traveled the world as a motivational speaker, helping people take control of their destiny by learning to let go of past heartache, remove fear and doubt, recover from grief and to take joy in their success. There has been no greater pleasure for me than being able to help my audiences awaken to and appreciate the power of their lives, and my goal in writing this book is to incorporate all that I have shared with my in-person audiences with you. In reaching for this book you have begun a journey towards self-evaluation and expansion. If you are motivated to make the most out of your life, to avoid letting an opportunity pass you by or to simply be a bit more thankful for the people and events in your life, my mission will have been accomplished.

1

What is a moment?

Webster's Dictionary defines it in several ways: "A very short space of time," "a time of excellence or consciousness," and "a period of importance in influence or effect."

So clearly, though "moment" seems like a simple enough word, it can also be very powerful. Monumental things can happen in a very short period of time. Lives can change, fortunes can be made or lost, love can be found.

A moment, then, is a turning point—a point of reckoning—an awakening—a discovery. It is a highly personal matter and one that cannot be decided by someone else. It may involve career, friendship, love, even life or passing away. It is intensely private in the sense that it involves our feelings and our emotions. Yet, ironically, no matter how personal or private it is for us, our moment rarely, if ever, happens without other people in some way being involved.

So while your life's journey is indeed a process of self-discovery, at least on some level your interaction with other people does play a profound role in your moment. Someone gives you a job opportunity and your career is launched…your child is born and you feel a new sense of responsibility…someone smiles at you and you know you have found your soul mate. In each case, another person helps bring you to your moment.

It would appear that we are never too young to experience our moment. I had the pleasure of giving psychic readings to President Harry Truman. Much of the focus of the readings pertained to his political career and (surprisingly enough) his belief in the spirit world. But perhaps nearest and dearest to his heart was his love for wife Elizabeth "Bess" Virginia Wallace. It would seem that, in the case of Harry Truman, it was possible to know, even as a young child, when true love had been found.

A series of chance meetings brought these two together. It began in 1890 when he was six and she was five. They met in Sunday school kindergarten at the First Presbyterian Church in Independence, Missouri. Young Harry was instantly drawn to her but too shy to approach her. They went on to attend separate elementary schools and one would imagine their lives would never again be intertwined.

A few years later, the Truman family moved to a new house and Harry began attending Columbian School. Surprisingly, one of his new classmates was none other than Bess Wallace—the same young Bess he had admired as a small boy. They began a friendship and later a romance and finally, after another series of separations, married in 1919.

Truman's cousin, Ethel Noland, went through school with Harry and Bess and was quoted as saying, "There never was but one girl in the world for Harry Truman, from the first time he ever saw her at the Presbyterian kindergarten." (*How they Met,* Black Dog and Leventhal Publishers 2003). And Margaret Truman, in her book *Bess W. Truman* (Macmillan Publishing Company 1986), said, "… six-year-old Harry Truman walked into the classroom of the First Presbyterian Church and saw a 'little blue-eyed, golden-haired girl' named Bess Wallace. To the end of his life, he insisted that he fell in love with five-year-old Bess on the spot."

Clearly, that one enchanted moment when they first met as children shaped their destiny as a couple. Imagine the impact—the force—of such a meeting. Two lives were bound together forever by that single instant. And little did they know at their tender ages the many milestones they would share in the future. He became a senator from Missouri. Later, the two of them became the thirty-third President and First Lady of their country.

Another love story involves the late actress Beverly Garland and her husband of many years. Beverly had a long and impressive career, having appeared in films and in recurring roles in many television series such as *My Three Sons, Remington Steele, Scarecrow and Mrs. King, Lois & Clark, Port Charles* and *7th Heaven.*

But her moment involves not her career but love, all the more tender and precious because it almost eluded her. She wrote her recollections of her moment not long before her passing:

My husband changed my life.

I met Fillmore Pajeau Crank on a blind date. I thought he was very handsome and that he had a good mind. But I felt a spark was missing. We went out a few times and then I decided to call it off.

My good friend (who had introduced us) asked him to bring me to her birthday party...so I decided to try one more time. That night I really thought it might be a good idea to give this man the benefit of my doubt. I found I could talk to him for hours and he never bored me. I found I loved the way his mind worked. I found he was one of the most honest men I had ever met. His friends thought highly of him. And I learned they also thought him to be special.

His wife had been killed in an auto accident and he had two children. They were twelve and sixteen. He was trying very hard to raise them by himself. I kept learning about this man, this Mr. Crank, and decided as time went by not to ever let him go.

Needless to say he never stopped giving and made my thirty-nine years of marriage a treasure. He died of primary liver cancer after thirty-nine years of a unique marriage. We raised his children and had two of our own.

He lives in my heart and will always.
I was blessed.
My husband changed my life.

How fortunate that Beverly did not give up, but instead gave a second chance to a man who might otherwise have stayed only a friend, if even that. That one act of attending her friend's birthday party truly turned the tide.

Beverly's story so beautifully tells us that love is not necessarily comprised of "bells and whistles" at first. It may come about in a simple, gentler way, but it is nonetheless life-altering when it arrives.

Perhaps you have wondered about the wisdom in beginning a relationship with someone who has children from a prior marriage. Maybe you have feared the risks or responsibilities involved. I psychically feel that somewhere in her heart, whether she knew it or not, Beverly may have had a similar hesitation. She may have wondered whether she was up to the task of taking on a new relationship and children.

But obviously the rewards were worth any risks. This charming woman allowed her heart to take a chance and she, Fillmore and their children became an adoring new family.

Love really was lovelier the second time around.

There is one additional love story to mention: the romantic couple of Rudy and Eleanor Vallee. Before there was Elvis Presley, Frank Sinatra, Bing Crosby or Michael Jackson, there was Rudy Vallee—a true legend in the music business. Women swooned over the "Vagabond Lover" as he was known. He came into prominence in the 1920s and held court on radio, stage and film for many years.

His marriage to Eleanor might never have happened had they paid attention to conventional wisdom or public opinion. Ellie, as I know her, was a teenager when they met. Rudy was a middle-aged man. Ellie describes their meeting, and her moment, this way:

> *The most exciting moment of my life was when I met Rudy Vallee. I was fifteen years old at Kings Beach, Lake Tahoe, California. I was in a two-piece bathing suit, and had long red hair. It was a wonderful day—what a memory—never to forget! Then, I met my future husband, "Rudy Vallee."*

What followed was a courtship where on several dates Ellie's parents were also included. But they finally dated solo and soon became a couple deeply in love. To many, the age difference would have been frightening or unthinkable. But to Rudy and Ellie, it simply did not matter because their love was so strong. Had they tried to fight it, a truly great romance might never have happened.

In her book, *My Vagabond Lover* (Taylor Publishing Company, 1996), Ellie says:

> *My role was that of a traditional wife who gave up any thought of career to be with her man. I make no apologies for accepting this role. Rudy was my full-time career and I never wanted to change a moment of it. Once I had fallen in love with him, I put all thoughts of a separate career behind me. I adored Rudy and everyone knew it. I admit perhaps I am old-fashioned. I wanted to be with my husband at all times…Rudy and I were a unit. While we both kept our individuality, we were life partners.*

I knew Rudy for many years and always considered him to be one of the most charismatic men in show business. I first met him after seeing him perform at the Mark Hopkins Hotel in San Francisco. And I consider Ellie a treasured friend to this day.

All of the couples mentioned prove that finding love can clearly be a powerful and emotional moment. In fact, I have yet to encounter anyone who has told me that their moment was special because it made them rich or famous, even though that may have been the end result. Instead, people recall a moment because it produced an emotional response. True, on the surface, a moment may enhance or better our life. But what makes the moment memorable is the emotional response we feel. What make us unique, and what make our life worthwhile, are our feelings and our emotions.

A robot could achieve something. It could win a race. But the robot would not derive any satisfaction from winning. It would not mean anything to the robot. The robot could not savor the victory or sense the accomplishment. And there would be no motivation for the robot to keep winning. The win would be nothing more than a physical act. The physical is important, but it means little without the addition of emotions.

Undoubtedly, a six-year-old Harry Truman may not have been emotionally mature enough to ask for a soul mate. But this brings up an interesting point. It is a common practice, during prayer or meditation, to ask for what we want. And many times, we receive it. But in some instances, it seems we can pray or meditate very intensely or over a long period of time without receiving what we have asked for.

I ask you to consider the possibility that you are not meant to receive exactly what you are asking for. The timing may be wrong or the person or thing you desire may be wrong for you.

I once sold a home and was unable to find another home by the time escrow had closed. I moved into an apartment for what I thought would be a temporary period of time. For the next seven years I searched in vain for a permanent home. It began to feel like an almost impossible mission and I found myself asking, "Why am I not able to find a home? What am I doing wrong?"

Then one day, I was on yet another round of house hunting with my broker and this time my co-author Valerie was along as well. We were driving away after having seen another inappropriate home. We began to pass another residence and Valerie said, "Wait! Stop here! Kenny—look at this home!"

I did look and then said, "That's the perfect-looking home from the exterior!" The broker pointed out that there was no "FOR SALE" sign out front.

"Can you check your records when you get back to your office?" I asked. "I feel this home is available."

The next day my broker called. "You're right!" she chuckled. "It was just listed for sale, but the family prefers not to have a sign out front since they don't live nearby and don't want to flaunt the fact that the home is vacant."

The long and the short of the story, Sweet Spirit, is that this has been my home for the past 17 years now! This is the answer to why my search for a home had taken so long. The home that was meant for me had not been available previously.

I believe so strongly that a higher force was at work and that this higher force knew that my rightful home would come along. What I *wanted* was to find a home quickly. But what I *needed*—a safe home, a happy home—took a bit longer to come along.

We get sidetracked asking for what we want, when we want it, instead of asking for what we need, when we are meant to receive it. Great care and wisdom go into that decision.

There is a conclusion to my story about house hunting that proves how the timing truly was appropriate and nothing short of miraculous. Within mere months of moving into my home Southern California was rocked by a severe E-a-r-t-h-q-u-a-k-e (I prefer not to use the actual word but to spell it out instead, so as not to give it energy). Yet there was no damage to my new home whatsoever. In driving past my previous neighborhood, I found that the street where I had lived was very badly damaged and the apartment complex itself was nearly demolished. I shudder to think of the loss to personal property and perhaps the injury that I could have experienced had I still been living there. So, indeed, I left at the right time.

Furthermore, in the weeks following the quake I had occasion to drive through several of the neighborhoods where I had searched for homes in years gone by, past the location of many actual homes I had often considered buying but which sale had never materialized for one reason or another. Entire homes and often large portions of the streets were lost and my loss would have been among them. I said prayers for those who had suffered through this devastation and said another prayer of thanksgiving that I had been blessed not with what I *wanted* but with what I *needed*.

As I mentioned previously, we have preconceived ideas of what we want and what we think is best for us. In some cases our instincts are right and we do indeed receive what we long for. But in other cases, despite our hard work and determination, despite our faithful meditation or prayers, things do not seem to turn out the way we want them to. This is when we should step back and re-evaluate. It is entirely possible that the reason we have not received what we have been asking for is because something even better is in store for us. Perhaps what we should have been doing all along is focusing on our desires, working towards what we think we would like, but also saying, "This is what I want…IF it is for my good and if it is indeed what is best for me, so that everything is in Divine Order."

Your moment may come about in numerous ways. It may come after careful planning, in just the way you had hoped. Then again, it may come out of the blue from a source that is totally unexpected. Ultimately, what matters is that, in the end, your best interests were met.

I would like to share an example of a moment that came about in a completely unexpected way.

While talking on the telephone one day with legendary screen star Debbie Reynolds, I asked her to describe her moment for inclusion in this book. She told me how she had been born Mary Frances Reynolds in El Paso, Texas, "dirt poor" as she described it. She said when she was six years old her father moved to California to get steady work with the railroad and a year later the family (Mary Frances, her mom, and her brother) followed. They settled in Burbank, near Warner Brothers Studios.

The story she told me was one of determination, incredible good luck and most importantly, keeping one's word. It was the story of how Mary Frances Reynolds was "discovered." "But, Kenny," she explained, "I said it best in the book I wrote" (*Debbie*, Pocket Books 1988). To fully illustrate her moment she gave me permission to share excerpts with you here:

> *One May day in 1948, my friend Norma Harris and I were walking down Magnolia Boulevard when we saw a little handbill advertising the Miss Burbank contest that was being sponsored by Lockheed Aircraft. Every girl who entered, it said, no matter what, received a blouse and a scarf. All you had to do was enter and they gave you a scarf and a blouse?! The only requirement was that the girls had to be sixteen or over. I made it by a month! We hurried right over to the Recreation Hall to sign up.*
>
> *It seemed like half the girls in my class were there registering— the pretty half, that is. After all, it was a beauty contest. But that didn't matter to me. I didn't tell anybody, but I never dreamed of going through with it. I was not exactly a member of the glamour department; I didn't even wear lipstick. What did matter was getting the white silk sports blouse and a green scarf.*
>
> *Plus, we were all going to be taken someplace for a free lunch! A party!*
>
> *My mother thought we were crazy when we told her.*
>
> *"Miss Burbank?!" She couldn't believe there was such a thing.*

The night of the contest, we were sitting at the dinner table when Mother brought it up. I thought she'd forgotten.

"What time you supposed to be down at the auditorium, Mary Frances?"

"Oh, I'm not going till about eight-thirty."

"What? Isn't that starting a little late?"

"Well, it doesn't matter for me because I'm not going to be in it," I answered blithely.

"What? How come?"

"Well, because…I'm not going to go enter some beauty contest! I'm not that dumb."

"You were dumb enough to sign up and collect the free blouse and scarf and the lunch!" she reminded me reproachfully.

My father said, "Sis is going to be in a beauty contest? You kiddin' around?" he asked Mother. He wasn't putting me down. He just saw it as another one of my jokes.

"I don't know, but she signed up to be in it."

"Oh Mother, Daddy's right," I said. "It's silly for me to do that. For one thing, it's wasting their time."

"That's not the point, Mary Frances."

But then my father said, "Oh, no, you don't. You gave your word. Anytime a Reynolds gives his word, he keeps it."

"Well, I can't go. I got a hole in my bathing suit."

"Well, I'll sew up the hole in your bathing suit," Mother said, "but you're gonna go."

So that was it. Yes, sir. Yes, ma'am.

And so Mary Frances went to the pageant, keeping her word as her parents had taught her. For the talent portion, she decided to do a Betty Hutton impersonation, as she had previously done in the Girl Scouts. The girls were each asked a few questions about themselves:

Then came the talent. There were girls with beautiful voices; one girl played the harp. Another did a tap dance. Another acted out a scene from Little Women. I stood back in the wings watching. Each girl was better than the last.

I came out lugging my record player, balancing precariously in high heels. I almost fell over with my backside to the audience as I placed the record player on the floor. There was a big laugh out front. I realized they thought I had planned it. So I turned around and said, "I'm wearing heels for the first time in my life and they're killing me. May I take them off?"

They loved it! They started clapping and shouting, yelling "Yes!" at me. It was just like the Girl Scouts for this natural-born ham. I went into my Betty Hutton routine in comfort, performing "I'm a Square in the Social Circle."

When I finished they hooted and stomped. I packed up my things and left the stage, barefooted, high heels balanced on top of the record player.

I was walking out the stage door with my things when the man from the Chamber of Commerce stopped me.

"Where you going, Mary Frances?"

"Home," I answered.

"Oh, you gotta stay till it's over," he said. "Those are the rules."

And so, once again learning to keep true to her word, Mary Frances stayed. To her surprise and delight, she was announced the winner of the contest. She won a robe and pajama set, a string of pearls and a trip for two to New York, all expenses paid.

But her most important "win" was yet to come, for in the audience serving as judges had been Solly Baiano from Warner Brothers and talent scout Al Trescone from MGM Studios. Unbeknownst to young Mary Frances, both men had been intrigued with her and saw potential for her in the movies. They flipped a coin to see who would arrange a screen test first. Solly Baiano won and the next day, the Reynolds family received a call from Warner Brothers.

Mary Frances Reynolds did the screen test, was signed to a seven-year contract, had her name changed to Debbie, and began what would become a most impressive career, with roles in such classics as *Singin' in the Rain*, *The Unsinkable Molly Brown* and *How the West Was Won*.

Think of how that moment—deciding to enter the pageant and then most importantly, keeping her word to go through with the pageant appearance instead of just collecting the reward and moving on—changed her life. It gave her a marvelous career and gave the world so many incredible entertainment memories.

Debbie Reynolds was innocently seeking nothing more than new items of clothing and she gained so much more along the way. To attract what you desire and what is meant for you I suggest repeating a simple phrase such as "The job that I seek seeks me" or "The love that I seek seeks me." Fortunately, before finding my home, I learned to say "The home that I seek seeks me." And I firmly believe this to be true. If indeed something is right for you, the Universe will find a way for you to obtain it.

To me one of the most important factors in life is to believe in a higher power, whatever that may be for you. Learn to aim high, to dream big dreams and to believe that these dreams can in some way and somehow come true. Never give up hope, Sweet Spirit. Your needs may seem enormous to you. But to a higher force, which will be helping you, these needs are small in comparison to their capacity to fulfill those needs.

In many religions based on Christianity, there is the belief taken from the Bible that we should "Ask and it will be given to you; search and you will find; knock and the door will be opened for you." (Matthew 7:7).

This seems like solid advice no matter what your religious beliefs may be. Whether you are praying to a religious figure, a loved one whose spirit you are attempting to contact, or a higher force whose unseen presence you believe in, it is often helpful to turn to these outside forces to ask for what you desire, expecting that your needs will be fulfilled.

But bear in mind that believing in a higher force or plan implies that we are not in total control of our lives—our destiny. For many people, this is an easy concept to accept. While I certainly believe in a higher force, I also believe that we have an element of free will and we do have some control over the choices we make and the lives we lead.

I believe that we are given clues to the opportunities that await us and it is up to us to follow those clues. In the spiritual world we refer to these clues as "omens" or "apports." An example of an omen might be hearing a song on the radio that contains a message or name that provides an answer to a question you have or gives validation to something you have been curious about. Or, suppose you are wondering whether to take a vacation or move to a new location and you look at the license plate of a car driving in front of you. The license plate reads OK 2 GO. That is an omen—it gives you a clue to move ahead with your plans.

An apport is a physical item that gives a clue or message to you. For example, you are debating whether to sign a lease on a condo on the third floor and you find three pennies while taking a walk near the condo. That is physical confirmation that the number three is significant to you. And no doubt the confirmation is a good sign.

No matter how self-sufficient we may think we are, the truth is that rarely do we work alone, without any outside influence or help. There is always someone who helped us along the way. It may have been a friend, a co-worker or even a person whose acquaintance we have barely made. Anyone can play a role in helping us accomplish our goals and attain important milestones in our lives. And anyone who has helped us would enjoy knowing that their efforts were appreciated.

I believe in the spirit world so in addition to thanking those people I encounter on Earthplane, I take time out to thank those dear ones in spirit, too, for watching over me and guiding me. I like to think that this makes them happy and more excited to help me in the future. I further believe that it helps this guardian angel's own spiritual growth because spirits, too, have a purpose and can make progress on the other side by being of help to others.

I urge you to remember to express gratitude for goals accomplished and wishes fulfilled. Asking for a favor is part one of the process. But part two is equally important and that is the art of being grateful for the granting of the favor. If you pray or meditate, return to that source with your words of thanksgiving.

Now, granted, not everything that happens can be seen as monumentally important. Our lives will not contain an unlimited amount of moments where major goals are achieved. We must not look only for the major events in our lives and overlook the simplest of events, because these simple events can often have a great impact, too.

Perhaps you think you have nothing to be thankful for. You may be unhappy with your current job, for example. But remember that you *have* a job, dear one, and somewhere there is a person wishing hard for that very thing. You may wish that you were in better health. You have every right to want improved health for yourself or a loved one. But take a walk through a hospital and see the many cases worse than yours will ever be.

Appreciate all of life! You will never get yesterday back again. You will never hear anyone say, "Yes, I did it tomorrow." The endearing though perhaps clichéd advice to "stop and smell the roses" is indeed true. It is fairly common to look back in time days, weeks or even years after an event has occurred and think, "I didn't realize it then, but that really was a wonderful time!" How truly powerful it would be if we could learn to appreciate events and people now, while they are a part of our life.

A happy moment can arise from something seemingly minute. If you have ever had a loved one or perhaps a beloved pet suffer an illness and then suddenly eat a full meal or take a walk, you know the joy that can come from such a simple pleasure. Take note of a long talk with a parent or sibling, a game played with a child or a pet, your own achievement in getting dressed following an illness or making a bank deposit after months of unemployment. Happy moments can be simple indeed.

And yet, as special as they may be, these would certainly be classified as "sub-moments" in the grander picture of life, much as there are sub-titles in books or films.

Several people, when I spoke to them about this book, told me, "Oh, I've had too many moments to choose just one." Of course, I say "Congratulations!" I am delighted that they feel this way. But I contend that many of the times they were thinking of were sub-moments—intense and meaningful but not *the moment*.

I can only tell this from a psychic standpoint because in fact as I said no one can choose another's moment. But I would venture to say that while General Douglas MacArthur had many victories in his military life, each one important and satisfying, in the end his moment came when he was relieved of his command by President Harry Truman, because he disobeyed the President's order. This single instant clearly defined his life and certainly shaped his future (remember I mentioned that moments can appear to be good or bad).

There are some people, including perhaps a few who are reading this book, who would say, "I really don't have a moment. I can't think of any one thing or person that changed my life." I would say to those people, "Use your imagination; delve deeper into yourself!" To begin exploring your life in order to define your moment, sit quietly for a brief time. Say to yourself, "Let's go back to the first thing in my life that I can remember as being significant..." and then go on from there, swiftly but accurately reviewing your life. You will enjoy the process, I am quite sure, and along the way your one special moment will no doubt flash before you and you will gain a new appreciation for the person or event involved, and for your life in its total.

Regardless of your age, a new appreciation of and awareness of your life can begin again, all because of this trip back through time within your mind. You may recall something that has been buried deeply in your thoughts—a childhood experience, a friend you had all but forgotten. And even if this turns out not to be your one special moment you will have relived some wonderful memories along the way.

If you still cannot find a moment that you can define as your *true moment*, this might tell you something about yourself. You may need to take more risks, live life more fully. Perhaps you have been too safe with your emotions or the decisions you have made. Or it may be that your moment is yet to come, and that can be a delightful possibility to consider.

Remember, as you review your life's experiences, that this is about YOU. It is not about your mate, or your family. If it seems that I am encouraging you to become selfish in your thinking, you are absolutely right. It is precisely what I intend to do. For a brief time, focus on the inner you. No one can share your inner feelings; no one can live your life. In the process of your inner exploration, you may well find that you will become a more understanding person, a happier person, and a more contented person. This can only enrich your life and make you a better person in dealing with those around you.

One last thing to consider before moving on: It is entirely possible that YOU may be part of someone else's moment. You may play a role in this life-changing experience for someone else. Naturally, you cannot be expected to date everyone who has an interest in you, or marry everyone who asks, just to make another person happy. You certainly will not take every job that is offered to you or become a friend to the entire world. But whenever possible, give of yourself. Be kind; share a part of yourself with others. A friendly phone call, a warm smile, a word of encouragement or compassion can have an impact on someone else's life. What magical power there is in knowing that, when someone else searches inwardly to find their moment, thoughts of you may well be included.

2

Don't wait for life to happen to you

Perhaps you are among the few whose moment has yet to occur. Or better yet, you are one of the fortunate ones who has recognized your moment. Either way, there may be times when you hear of something wonderful happening to someone else and think, "I'd like to have that happen to me."

For even if you are eternally grateful for your moment and the many good things that have happened to you, it is likely that you will occasionally find yourself saying, "I'd like even more, please…more love, more happiness, more of everything that is good."

There is certainly nothing wrong with wanting more. There is a world of difference, however, between begrudging what someone else has to the point of envy, and being happy for them but wanting something for yourself that is similar. For example, I may like my co-worker's car. It does not, however, mean that I want *their* car or that I resent their having it. Instead, I set my mind on working hard to obtain a car *like* it—one that is clearly meant for me. And only I can help make this a reality. Being envious or simply wishing something were mine would get me nowhere.

What we want is not always an object. Sometimes it can be an emotion or a feeling. One of the most common desires lies solely within our own power to obtain. This is peace of mind. For years I have advised clients from all walks of life. They come to me for advice about issues including career, love and health. But I often find that the commodity they seek above all others is peace of mind.

Peace of mind is something that you cannot buy. True, you can pay for items that make you happy—a vacation, a car, a new home. But there is no price tag that can be placed on the actual feeling of peace of mind or the emotional satisfaction that comes with peace and contentment.

We can choose to find and create inner peace by taking a few minutes each day to relax in meditation, prayer or just quiet thought. There is always something to be grateful for—some glimmer of hope. Focus on that glimmer and it will begin to shine brightly. There is no need to wait for everything to be perfect in our lives in order to feel peace of mind. Some level of inner peace is attainable at all times, no matter what might be going on in the outside world. If you believe that there is a Divine plan somewhere in the works and that the Universe has a place for you and a master plan for you, then you know that what is happening at this moment is what is meant to be happening. The most that you can do, for your part, is to be sure you are doing all that you can to make your life the best it can be.

From time to time during my lectures or during private consultations, I try a little experiment that tells me whether someone is a "take charge" person or not. I will say to them, "You know the old saying—'God helps those who…'" and then I wait. If the person simply nods or says "Yes, I know," I know they are not as active as they can be. To me, the truly active and productive person will finish the phrase correctly, saying "…help themselves."

One such person who clearly recognized the instant when she could help herself is comedienne Jo Anne Worley. I have known Jo Anne for many years. She is perhaps best remembered by television audiences for her four years on the Emmy-winning series *Rowan & Martin's Laugh-In*, as well as countless guest appearances on several television series and game shows. She has also appeared frequently on stage in national companies of *Mame*, *Hello, Dolly!*, *Wicked*, *Gypsy* and many other productions.

Jo Anne has had an impressive nightclub career as well and credits a particular moment with bringing about her success. To me, her moment is a clear example of recognizing a time of opportunity and seizing it, instead of waiting for something to happen. Jo Anne truly helped create her success, as her story illustrates:

> *One of the major turning points in my life was when a small spotlight was left on me, when it should have been turned off. I had a very small part in a show starring Joey Faye and Jack Albertson. It was doing famous burlesque sketches, called "Laff Capades." This was my very first paid show in Hollywood—$5.00 a performance—at the Le Grande Comedy Theatre (which was the old Hollywood Canteen).*

> *I was in only one sketch and it was in the second act. It was pantomime, the ol' switching the poison drink routine. Billy Barnes happened to come to see the second act. He was a friend of Dee Arlen, who was the female lead in the show.*
>
> *During the bows, the lights went off on everyone except me. So I started mugging and got the audience laughing. It happened several times.*
>
> *After the show, Billy Barnes came backstage and asked if I talked. I, of course, replied, "Yes!" "Sing?" "Yes!" Could I "come in and audition for the second company of his show, which was going to Broadway?" "YES!"*
>
> *I did the show in Hollywood. The next show he did that went to Broadway, I was in it and I stayed in New York, where more wonderful things happened.*

Jo Anne's moment shows how important it is to be alert at all times and to seize an opportunity when we find it.

It is true that we are shown opportunities and given chances to improve our lives. But we must then take an active role in creating our best moments in life. For example, it is all well and good to say prayers for your good health. But while doing this, make sure you are not snacking on junk food, and that you are you doing your part to improve your health by exercising, eating properly and taking your vitamins or medications.

However much responsibility we take for our lives, we still cannot, or at least we should not, force things to go our way if in fact something else is in our best interest. It is impossible to force a moment by marrying someone whom we know in our heart is wrong, to have children because our friends are having them or to embark on a harmful habit because "everyone is doing it."

The secret is to do what makes you feel good about yourself rather than what you feel pressured to do by outside sources. If your hobby is not popular or your particular "look" is not the trendiest, it does not matter, as long as you are not harming anyone and you are creating happiness for yourself.

One man who made a decision to pursue what made him happy is Sam Simon, and because of this decision he has brought happiness to countless television viewers. Sam is a twelve-time Emmy winner and has written, produced and directed such television classics as *Taxi, Cheers, The Tracey Ullman Show, The Drew Carey Show* and *The Simpsons*, which he co-created. His moment ultimately led to this brilliant career, as he explains:

> I was always a class clown, but when I got to college I clammed up. I was killing myself studying, trying to get into a great law school. But I didn't even really want to go to law school. I had always been creative and funny, but I was miserable and depressed because I didn't have an outlet. My future seemed bleak.
>
> Then one day I arrived late for the first day of a class. It was being held at Dinkelspiel Auditorium, the biggest lecture hall at Stanford University. There were probably a thousand students in the class, and the only open seat was down front, in the middle of the third row.
>
> The professor stopped lecturing as I walked down the steps inside the auditorium. For what seemed like an eternity, I had to climb over other students as I made my way through the long, narrow row. "Excuse me…Excuse me…Excuse me…Excuse me…"
>
> The instant I sat down the professor made an announcement: "If there's anyone in this auditorium who is going to be late for another class, I suggest they get up and leave right now."
>
> Immediately, I got up and began making my way back out the row. "Excuse me…Excuse me…Excuse me…Excuse me…"
>
> The laughter built to a crescendo as I climbed back up the steps and left the auditorium.
>
> It felt great. I switched my priorities. I began spending most of my time drawing cartoons for the local newspapers and less studying for a life I would have hated. Were it not for that day, I doubt there would have been a "Simpsons."

I am sure the many fans of that show and the other shows that Sam added his creative touch to are glad that he switched his priorities, too. Instead of fighting what he truly was meant to do and what gave him the most pleasure, he decided to embrace it and make it his life's work. This was a simple moment that brought about a complete change in his life. And it can happen to any of us, if we are true to ourselves instead of doing what we feel is expected of us.

Not giving in to pressure from others is critical. But equally as important is resisting the temptation to impose our wishes and dreams on someone else. We are in no position to judge what is important to another person. You may like jazz while I like show tunes. That in no way makes me "right" and you "wrong."

I had the pleasure of knowing a controversial woman who definitely pursued what she wanted regardless of what public opinion might have been. I will say she was one of the happiest and most well-adjusted people I have ever met.

The woman I am referring to is Christine Jorgensen, the first person to have complete sex reassignment surgery. Christine was born George Jorgensen, Jr. The Bronx-born George served two years in the Army. After his discharge he began hormone treatments and a total of six surgeries in Denmark until finally becoming Christine, a striking-looking blonde woman, in 1952.

I met her through Gretchen Fine, a publicist friend of mine. Gretchen was representing Christine, who was in demand for personal appearances and lectures. Gretchen brought Christine to a birthday party I gave for my mom Kaye in Beverly Hills.

There were many celebrated personalities such as Regis Philbin in attendance. Since so many in the room were well known themselves, there was no stargazing. This was basically a room full of friends.

Yet when Gretchen and her guest walked in and I said, "Oh, Gretchen, how nice of you to bring Christine Jorgensen!" all eyes turned to look and you could hear loud whispers. Christine became the center of attention. Far from being embarrassed by the attention she seemed to bask in it.

I would imagine, though of course I cannot speak for her, that Christine's moment was when she shed the outer shell of her life as George and became, once and for all, the woman she felt she was meant to be.

I asked Gretchen what her own moment was and not surprisingly, she said:

One of the high points of my life was knowing and representing Christine Jorgensen, who became a real friend as well as a real person who never took herself seriously.

Chris had a great sense of humor and was a very knowledgeable individual and she was one of my very favorite people in my life.

Christine passed at the age of sixty-two in 1989, but I am quite sure that she thoroughly enjoyed the years of her life following her transformation. Gretchen spoke of Christine's sense of humor and I can attest to that. I asked her one time what types of questions she was asked when she did her lecture tours, often on college campuses.

"Well, the most frequent question I'm asked is if I can have an orgasm," she smiled.

"And how do you answer that?" I asked.

She laughed and said, "I tell them 'you bet I can!'"

This delightful woman never let anyone persuade her away from her dream or force her to live a life she did not want.

We are not in a position to determine what someone else's moment is, nor can we determine when or how it will happen.

Many a parent has learned that they can steer a child in a particular direction for schooling or a career. But if the child shows no aptitude or interest in that field, there seems little point of continuing down that path.

Living in Southern California I have encountered many women who are labeled "stage mothers" because they are aggressively pushing their children into a career in the entertainment business. Now, in many cases, the term "stage mother" has developed a negative connotation because of the aggression and determination the parent exhibits. But often this word is incorrectly used to describe a parent who is merely taking an active interest and role in helping their child study or pursue a show business career. The parent should instead simply be called supportive, if they are offering encouragement to a child whose desire to succeed in show business is strong. After all, it would be impossible for the child to even accomplish something as basic as getting to the audition without an adult such as their parent to drive them.

Many children have subsequently decided not to pursue a lifelong entertainment career but have first saved money for a college education from their earnings in show business, thanks to understanding and supportive parents.

The mistake comes when a child does not want to act or sing and has it repeatedly forced upon them by a parent who probably is vicariously living through them, making up for the show business career they wish they had been able to attain.

Every field has "stage mothers and fathers" in a sense. By that I mean that they are well-meaning parents pushing their children to become doctors or lawyers when the children would much rather be engineers or landscapers.

The best thing that can happen to a person is to pursue to the fullest the thing which they desire the most, using every method possible to achieve a goal. To use a military example, I have always believed in going to "the General" for an answer. In other words, my advice would be to refuse to take "no" as an answer from someone who is really not in the position to tell you yes or no. Suppose one secretary or receptionist tells you that there are no appointments available with a personnel manager at a firm where you would like to work. But you have only received an answer from that one person. Find a way to reach another person, preferably the personnel manager directly. Try phoning again, write a letter, send a fax. Be creative and persistent in your techniques.

When you think of the name Frank Sinatra, you may automatically think of a legend who one day burst upon the entertainment scene as a star and stayed a star till the end of his life. If so, the following story of one of the encounters I had with him may surprise you. And even if you happen to know the inside facts which I am about to relay, you will certainly come to the conclusion that Frank Sinatra was the epitome of persistence and a master at making the most of a moment, by going to "the General":

I was in Palm Springs in 1972 and had tickets for a showing of Francis Ford Coppola's classic film *The Godfather*, which had recently opened to rave reviews. The Plaza Theatre on Palm Canyon Drive was selling advance tickets for the film and after purchasing them for an evening screening my mom, her friend and I decided to pop next door to the famed (and unfortunately now-defunct) Louise's Pantry restaurant for a bite to eat. But we had no sooner ordered when I excused myself, saying to the ladies, "I have to go across the street for a couple of minutes—I have a psychic impression and I'm being sent across the street." I left Mom and her friend and started across Palm Canyon, without any real clue as to why.

I soon saw a Rolls-Royce parked on the street, with the license plate "FAS" and then I knew what my psychic "mission" was. I had been curious about the health of Frank Sinatra, since it had been rumored for some time that he was having a problem involving his hand. I put two and two together, recognizing that the license plate of "FAS" was an abbreviation for Francis Albert Sinatra, and it made sense that he would be driving a Rolls-Royce. A moment later I saw him coming out of a nearby shop.

I approached him, calling out "Frank!" We'd never met and he rather indignantly responded, "Yes?" I quickly said, "I'm sorry—Mr. Sinatra. I'm Kenny Kingston - a friend of Jim Bacon." James Bacon was a highly respected columnist syndicated in about 450 newspapers around the country, and a friend of Frank Sinatra's and countless other performers. Mentioning our mutual friend put Sinatra at ease and he greeted me more warmly.

I wondered to myself, "Is he really still having a problem with his hand, or is it healed?" and put the question to the test, reaching out to shake the once-afflicted hand. He responded with a firm handshake and we more properly said "hello." I smiled and knew the question had been answered. I said I was happy to see he was doing better, and that I would relay this information to Jim Bacon when I talked to him next. "Yes," he smiled, "you do that!"

Since I had mentioned being happy about his condition, I continued the conversation by asking him what event made him happiest (little did I know that I would be working on this book many years later). He said he had certainly felt love in his life and his children had made him happy, but continued, "Kenny, I've gotta tell you, the happiest and most satisfying moment was when I signed the contract to do *From Here to Eternity*."

Sinatra explained that while he'd been a singing sensation and had conquered the music world, he nevertheless hit an inevitable slump that many in show business experience, no matter how powerfully successful they might have been. "Then I heard of the part of Angelo Maggio in *From Here to Eternity*," he said, "and I pleaded with the powers-that-be to give me the role." It seems that the only person who envisioned Sinatra in the role at the time was Sinatra himself! But he was persistent, taking a relatively small salary in order to make casting him in the role even more appealing.

The persistence paid off and Sinatra's portrayal won the 1953 Best Supporting Actor Oscar. The role also brought his career into prominence again, with an added dimension. His talent as an actor was taken seriously and he appeared in several additional films.

It all began with him finding the right moment to talk to the right person (director Fred Zinnemann) and then convincing this top person that he was the right person for the role. As I said, it really is all about going to "the General."

Sometimes "the General" may not be a person at all, but merely symbolic. It primarily represents giving your best effort to each situation. Try taking one approach towards achieving your goal. If that method is not successful, try another and another—again and again if necessary. If you have done all that you can, if you truly feel that you have spoken to every person you can think of, then you may have to aim for something slightly different as a goal. Certainly we do not always succeed at everything we put our mind to. But make sure that you can truly tell yourself that you have taken every path towards a goal before abandoning or revising it.

If you feel you have really given something your best effort then there should be no sense of failure in revising a plan, either by choice or necessity. Sometimes the road you end up taking may be even more exciting than the one you set out to take. Know in your heart that you are making the most of every opportunity and view each achievement, no matter how seemingly insignificant, as a stepping stone toward your ultimate goal.

Being persistent in pursuit of your goals is an important aspect toward achieving happiness. But it is by no means the only key to success. Being truthful to oneself and staying true to your values is equally vital, in either your business or personal life. Valuing yourself enough to be who you are is a prime ingredient. Your happiness—the peace of mind we mentioned—must come from within. It is not dependent upon outside circumstances or other people.

Too many times I have counseled women who say that they know they would be happier if they saw their boyfriends more often, but they feel their boyfriends are not truly in love with them because they need to lose ten pounds. Men have said they think their wife would appreciate them more and their marriage would be better if they got a promotion at work. How easy it is to look to someone else to make us happy, and to expect outside situations to fulfill us inwardly.

We have probably all heard a friend say at one time or another that they had a terrible weekend because they were without a date. Perhaps you have said your vacation was ruined because you were unable to meet anyone special. Sweet Spirit, a vacation alone or with a non-romantic friend can be a golden opportunity to explore a side of yourself you may have never explored before. There might be a museum you have wanted to see or a cooking class being offered at the hotel where you are staying. For Heaven's sake—and for your OWN sake, don't miss out on this opportunity because you are feeling sorry for yourself that you are not having a romantic encounter. Quite possibly, you are being given the time to explore something that you would otherwise not have had a chance to explore. And for all you know, your soul mate might be attending the same class or visiting the same museum, for people with like interests are often drawn to similar locations. If you meet that soul mate, so much the better…consider it a bonus along the way. But you might never meet that soul mate if you stick to only the traditional methods of having a drink in the hotel bar or going to a club late at night.

Sometimes we are required to step out of the ordinary—to back away from what is most comfortable, in order to be led to something that is wonderfully new and exciting. Eating the same type of food, visiting the same stores or restaurants, taking a vacation to the same familiar area may feel good. And if feeling good and feeling safe is your primary goal, congratulations. But we need never stop growing and expanding our horizons and our interests, if we choose to do so. Perhaps that change in plans or directions is just what you need.

If you are at home alone on a weekend, why not read that novel your friends have been talking so much about, catch up on a project you have wanted to undertake around your home. Take care of YOU; take care of your surroundings for a pleasant change of pace.

The more I see of today's modern inventions and our dependence on them, the more I worry about what it says about our opinion of ourselves. We spend countless time on our cell phones—time that used to be quiet time or alone time. People talk on their phones while shopping, waiting in line at the post office, and even while driving (even though it is against the law in many states). I was recently in a restaurant and recall seeing two people having dinner with one another but talking into their cell phones instead of to each other.

I would hate to think that people are so uncomfortable with themselves that they are afraid to spend time in their own company.

I applaud married couples who maintain their own identities as individuals, instead of feeling the need to do everything as a couple, unless of course they choose to do everything together. Spending occasional time apart should only increase the happiness as a couple because each person has spent quality time doing something they personally choose to do to enrich their lives. If a wife loves gardening and the husband wants to play golf, there is certainly no harm in that. Or for that matter, the reverse would be just as acceptable.

In fact it provides for more conversation when couples do get together if they have things to catch each other up on—"You'll never guess what I did today!" "Tell me what flowers you planted."

In the end, many activities are solitary anyway. True, you can visit an art gallery or go to a movie with a companion. You can even read passages from the newspaper or a book to someone. But your reaction to the film or the book or the art is meant to be an individual experience. No amount of dependence on someone else's reaction can make your personal reaction any richer. It is meant to be a very intensely personal and solitary experience.

Your inward experiences and values are what will cause you to appreciate your life. Having said that, it is only normal for outward appearances to matter to some degree. So if something about your appearance or your living quarters disturbs you, by all means change it—improve it. If you honestly want it for yourself and it truly makes you feel better towards yourself, go for it!

But make sure you are changing for the right reasons. If you admire a quality or style in someone, and feel you would be equally attractive with that quality or in that style, adapt it to fit yourself and your lifestyle. If you feel another person's hairstyle is becoming on them and you have a similar shape of face or similar coloring, then by all means try a version of that hairstyle on yourself. But do it because you feel it will enhance YOU, not because you want to look like the other person or to be the other person. Instead, choose to be the best, and to look the best that you can.

It may well be true that imitation is the sincerest form of flattery. But I once spoke to my friend and client, famed Hollywood gossip columnist Hedda Hopper, about actors maintaining their individuality. She told me she despised hearing an aspiring actor say, "I've been told I look a lot like Humphrey Bogart." She said, "I tell them, you don't look like anyone. You look like you, and don't ever forget it! Don't try to be anyone else but you and you'll go much farther in this town!"

If you are setting out to improve your appearance in the hopes of improving your life, make sure your changes are made because you want them to be made, since the answer to your problems cannot always be found by changing outside appearances. For example, losing weight in and of itself will not make you a better or a kinder person; it will only make you a thinner person. And if at some point you gain back the weight you are no less in quality as a person for having done so.

I advise people not to label someone with negative terms such as fat, alcoholic, or drug addict. This sets a dangerous mental tone and automatically paves the way for what is perceived of as failure. How much better it is to say someone (including yourself) overeats occasionally, drinks excessively sometimes or abuses drugs from time to time.

Out of the darkest moment can come brilliant happiness if we allow ourselves to accept this as a possibility. Nowhere is it written that only success will come our way or that we will only experience good things all of our life. Sometimes our greatest triumphs come following our darkest hours, if we accept the fact that both success and the lack of it are all a part of our existence and that the important thing is to refuse to give up.

A clearcut example of this is the incredibly inspiring story of Helen Gurley Brown, Editor-in-Chief of *Cosmopolitan Magazine*, who wrote to me:

The moment—or perhaps five minutes—that changed my life impressively for the better was in 1960 when I was walking with my husband David Brown one Sunday morning. I told him I was about to be fired from my advertising job and might he think of a book I could write. He had helped other people do that. He said why didn't I write about being single...that I was like no other single woman he had ever met.

That was the beginning of my book, Sex and the Single Girl. *I didn't send out questionnaires or do any research, just wrote about myself and my friends. Sounds improbable but the book—and I'd never been published before—was a bestseller, stayed on the* New York Times *list for twenty-six weeks and became the basis for new* Cosmopolitan—*an old magazine that was dying but the management let me come in and try a new format.*

That was all those years ago and now there are forty-two editions of Cosmopolitan—*with my format—all over the world. I work with all of them. I think we'd have to say those moments in the park with my husband did change my life...still changed these forty-four years later!*

Helen may not have mentioned it, but in 1965 her book *Sex and the Single Girl* was made into a very popular movie starring Natalie Wood and Tony Curtis—yet another successful moment for her.

Most people would not immediately realize that being fired was the best thing that could have happened to them and yet this was exactly the case with Helen Gurley Brown. Her story tells us that we are all here for a good purpose, no matter what our situation might be currently or what it might have been in the past. There is always the possibility of a new horizon; there are always new abilities to be discovered. Her continued success more than forty years later is admirable and I believe that Helen is a role model to young people just beginning a career but wondering if they can "make it." She is also a fine example to people who may be at a crossroads, thinking they might be "failing" because their career has had a setback.

A new beginning is always around the corner from any ending. Reading about Helen's moment shows so beautifully the fact that just when a door seems to be closing, when things seem to be at their lowest, is when a new door—to a new venture—can open.

Think of the countless women's lives that have been touched and enriched by the new door that opened for Helen Gurley Brown.

If we can control our anxiety about tomorrow and let go of what seems to be a disappointment or negative turn of events, we can see that a higher force, somewhere in the Universe, will indeed help take care of us and bring us to our rightful place.

3

What a difference a day made

There is a classic song that begins with the lyric, "What a difference a day made, twenty-four little hours…" and that statement is far more than a lyric in a song. It is one of the truest sentiments to be found, in my opinion.

Think about the sometimes overwhelming difference that can take place in the space of a single day or for that matter, an hour, or even a minute. Lives have been changed in the time it takes to respond with a "yes" or "no," to answer a telephone or doorbell, to decide to go somewhere or stay home.

Saying "yes" to a marriage proposal forever affects the lives of two people and certainly saying "no" has a similarly dramatic effect.

I have personally had experience with what a difference saying "yes" or "no" can mean. I had said "no" to several talk shows that had contacted me to appear around Halloween (always a popular time for discussions on the psychic world). It was difficult to say "no" because I love working, but previous commitments kept me from appearing.

I'll admit that one or two psychics who were lesser known at the time benefited from my decision, because they not only appeared on the shows I had been offered, but went on to do other shows as well. So my saying "no" had long-range good effects for them.

Was I unhappy about this? Only in the sense that it is my nature to want to "do it all" and this was one time I couldn't. But I truly believed there was a reason for it and that some greater good was ahead for me.

Immediately after completing my prior engagements, I received a call to begin a psychic hotline and tape a series of television infomercials to promote it. This seemed like a wonderful opportunity to reach out to millions of people who might not yet be aware of the psychic world. It was also a chance to offer them psychic readings by one of the psychics we would hire to answer calls for that hotline.

Now, it is certainly possible that I might have been able to do both the infomercial and the talk shows that I had turned down. But I tend to believe instead that the infomercial was provided to me by my spirit guides who wanted to "console" me for the work that I missed out on. They wanted me to be able, this time, to say a resounding "yes" to something even more fulfilling than what I had been forced to say "no" to earlier.

It was a tremendous consolation which lasted seven years and brought psychic advice, education and entertainment into the homes of countless viewers.

I have a client who also had an experience with a moment that started out unpleasantly but had a wonderful outcome. She came to me sobbing one evening because she had just broken up with her boyfriend. "It's the worst time of my life," she sighed, "and it all happened because of a chance encounter—it all changed in an instant!" She told me that her boyfriend of three years had informed her that he needed to break their dinner date because he was going out of town to be with his mother who was ill.

Feeling sorry for herself and missing her boyfriend, she invited a girlfriend to have dinner with her at the restaurant where she was supposed to have dined with her boyfriend. "Would you believe it?" she cried. "Halfway through dinner, I saw my friend looking toward the restaurant's entrance and her expression changed dramatically. I asked her, 'What is wrong?' and then I turned to see for myself. I saw my boyfriend walking in, laughing and happily holding hands with a beautiful young woman!"

She told me, "I'll never trust anyone again." But I told her that because this man was unfaithful, it was not an indication that every one of the male species would be the same. "He wasn't even a true friend to you, let alone anything deeper," I explained. "He was perhaps an acquaintance of long standing, but nothing more." I assured her that a more meaningful relationship was in her future, with a very loyal man. "I can't believe it," she said.

With each visit to me, she insisted that I must be wrong about a new man in her life. Then one evening, she arrived for her reading smiling brightly. "I think you may be right," she laughed. "A really handsome and kind man has asked me out and I found myself saying yes to him!"

Without relaying any more details, suffice to say that a year later, she married the man and they now have a young son together. Out of a very painful moment came a "yes" that led to a date followed by potentially a lifetime of happiness.

Here is another example of the difference a moment can make: Let us imagine a scenario involving a young man named Matt. He moves to New

York hoping for a career in the theatre. Our fictional Matt is six feet tall, dark-haired, muscular, with an unusual voice. Matt takes a job waiting tables at a restaurant and auditions whenever possible, hoping for a break.

After a few months Matt becomes discouraged and decides, "I'm not going to succeed with an acting career." He moves back home to Michigan. The day after he moves, a Broadway producer comes into the restaurant during what was Matt's shift, wondering to himself how long it will take him to fill the role in his new play. He needs a *tall, dark-haired man who's muscular and has an unusual voice*. This is, of course, the perfect description of Matt. But Matt gave up and went home—*one day too soon*.

Suppose our fictional Matt had stayed. He might have made an impression on the producer and gotten a chance at the role, had he not given up his dream so quickly. Had Matt's time been spent in positive thinking instead of negativity, the outcome might have been entirely different.

We have all heard of, or read about, examples of fate seemingly stepping in to alter a life. I recall an article in a newspaper where a woman's desk at work faced a large window that looked out at the street. She called in sick one day, which was rare for her to do. That very day a driver lost control of his car, smashing right through the window and demolishing the woman's desk. Because she was absent and not sitting at her desk, her decision to stay home very likely saved her life.

Following the terrorist attacks of 9/11 there were many stories of lives changed because someone unexpectedly was, or by some miracle was not, in one of the World Trade Center buildings. Think of all that can be altered but for the sake of a few minutes, an hour or a day.

I remember that while visiting a friend of mine in the hospital, I took a moment to sit quietly in the lobby. A woman came rushing up to me and said, "Oh thank you, Kenny Kingston! My sister is doing so much better today!"

I recognized the woman as someone I had seen two days before, standing outside the room next to the patient I was visiting. The woman and another female were discussing their patient, saying, "The doctor says she probably won't fully recover from the injuries, if she even recovers at all." I couldn't help overhearing and eventually couldn't stop myself from quietly interrupting. "Excuse me, Sweet Spirits," I found myself saying. "Please don't give up on your patient!"

"But she's our sister, and we've been told she may not live," one of the women cried.

I told them that I believed that many times a patient can rally, despite what their doctor says. "No one really can say when someone will live or pass. That's God's job—the Master's job. And even He is subject to change," I cautioned them. "Don't plant the seed of doubt that your sister won't live. Your negativity could be contagious. She might give up her will to live if she senses that even her dear sisters believe it's impossible for her to recover."

They thanked me and we all went back in to see our respective patients. Thankfully, they must have taken our brief talk to heart. I would like to think that in some small way it contributed to their sister's improvement.

While that story has a happy ending, there are indeed times when an instant is all it takes to make a drastic change that appears to be devastating. I was very impressed with *Vera Drake,* a heart-wrenching British film that I saw several years ago. It clearly illustrates how a life can change in a mere moment. Its central theme is abortion. But it is also a film about human nature on many levels and it illustrates what a difference one moment can make.

On one level we view a young woman paying a painful price for giving in to having sex because she felt pressured by a boyfriend. She becomes pregnant as a result of that one moment of supposed pleasure and then, out of fear, seeks an abortion. Vera Drake, played by the incredibly talented Imelda Staunton, comes to her rescue, so it would seem, by performing the abortion.

But tragedy follows and Vera, who is basically a hardworking woman who lives to help other people in any way possible, becomes a central figure in the tragedy. She truly believes she is performing a service that women might otherwise not be able to receive. But suddenly she finds herself, in one instant, going from a family dinner to police headquarters for questioning. The audience is left to wonder what might have happened if she had not met the young girl…if she had not done what she thought was the right thing to do to help another human being.

I made a rather dramatic prediction regarding a non-fictional British woman—Princess Diana. In 1991 the U.K.'s *Daily Star* newspaper contacted me to do aura readings for several prominent British people. They were planning a two-part series on me and on my aura reading abilities, to be followed by an offer they would make to readers to send in a photo and get a reading from me.

Part one of the series featured photos of several people perhaps known primarily to residents in the U.K.; in some instances, there were also photos of world-famous figures. I confess I was not aware of the identity of some of the people in the photos they sent but naturally I was instantly familiar with the most famous of them all, Princess Diana.

My aura reading for the Princess can be found in detail at my website, www.kennykingston.org, but I recall a couple of startling aspects. Most chilling of all was my observance that the Princess was suffering from a digestive disturbance (I actually said something much stronger but the Palace pressured the paper to change it).

My aura reading was printed before any admission had been made that the Princess suffered from the eating disorder known as bulimia. I also warned the Princess of her particular danger period in life—the months of July through November - and I cautioned her to stay away from fast-moving cars during this time. As we unfortunately know now, her tragic and fatal accident occurred in Paris during the month of *August* in a *fast-moving car.*

But an item in the aura reading that ties in to our discussion of the moment involved my prediction that Diana would do something for a moment's pleasure that she would regret a lifetime. During the very timeframe that I was giving the aura reading and it subsequently appeared in the *Daily Star*, Diana was allowing her friends to speak to author Andrew Morton, and indeed cooperating with him herself, for the book that would shock the world when it was released the following year (*Diana: Her True Story*).

While Diana may well have received a momentary pleasure from revealing her side of her life story, I have heard many people say they think this one act more than any other was the beginning of the end of her marriage to Prince Charles and her life as a royal.

This is not to say that we should shy away from taking chances or being bold enough to dream the seemingly impossible dream. But we must also be aware at all times of the consequences of our actions. Taking responsibility for our actions and realizing the consequences of them—good or bad—is a very important lesson we learn.

From time to time I encounter someone who wants a reading from me because they need answers, comfort and if possible, spirit contact, because a loved one or friend committed suicide. Unfortunately, I must tell them that suicide is not the choice that a responsible person makes. It is not the action of someone who cares about the consequences of his or her actions and the impact it will have on friends and family.

Certainly, we must send loving thoughts to those who have committed suicide, for their souls were troubled before and are probably more troubled now on the other side. Suicide solves nothing and actually presents a new element of pain in the spirit world.

Imagine walking into a popular restaurant and demanding immediate seating without a reservation. Think what it would be like to expect front row seats at a sold-out concert or sports event for which you have no tickets. There is no space for you—you are not expected. This is a minor example of what happens when someone takes his or her life. The spirit world is not ready for this person. There is no one to greet the soul; no plans are made for a happy reunion with loved ones because the timing is wrong.

Our lives are a gift—a gift not to be taken lightly. The body we have is not ours to destroy. There is a higher plan for the length of time we are to inhabit that body. The time when we leave is not up to us to decide. Thus, the person who commits suicide has not only in one moment of irrational thinking harmed those who mourn their actions on Earth, they have merely traded one level of despair for another where they personally are concerned.

Ultimately, of course, those who commit suicide can find peace and happiness. But it involves a long process and one that is not desirable. I had a client tell me once that he wanted to kill himself but lacked the courage to do so. I quickly told him that the real courage would come in living. The true strength of character would be proven by living through the temporary unhappiness and emerging victorious.

We have all suffered some level of sadness or dissatisfaction with our lives at some point. This is a natural part of living. As much as we practice positive thinking, things are bound to be less than perfect on occasion. But rather than giving in to total despair, we should take heart in the fact that as quickly as things can go from good to bad they can reverse again and go from sorrow to happiness. Do yourself a favor the next time you feel things starting to go wrong in your life. Work harder, keep as positive an outlook as possible and notice how quickly events can go from apparently bleak to unbelievably happy. Anyone who has all but given up hope that a loved one can recover from an illness only to hear the doctor say that the loved one is going to be fine knows what I mean.

It may be momentarily intriguing to look at instances in our lives and wonder "what if" or "if only." There is a certain slightly dangerous emotional charge in wondering how our lives might have played out had a certain event had a different outcome. Suppose, at a turning point, we had made a different choice or taken another cause of action. It may be intriguing to wonder, if we had made another decision, if things would have been better for us.

At times, however, "if only" becomes an excuse to keep our expectations low or to set up a barrier between ourselves and the success we deserve. "If only I were thinner," we justify, "I'd get more dates." "If only I had a better job I'd be happier."

At other times we consider the "if only" scenario in terms of what we feel we should have done. We wonder: "If only I'd been driving the car instead of having my husband drive we wouldn't have crashed"; "If only I'd gotten her to the doctor sooner she wouldn't have passed away"; "If only I'd accepted the promotion when it was offered to me I would have been president of the company by now." But, Sweet Spirit, thinking this way involves giving yourself far more power than you actually possess! You were not solely responsible for someone coming into the world, so you are certainly not responsible for their departure from this world. We think we wield much more power and have much more control than we actually do. True, we have responsibility for our actions but we are not responsible for the actions of the Universe.

It is tempting to dream about what might have been if circumstances had been different—if they had gone "the right way." But what *is* the "right way"? In the end, we are exactly where we should be, and things are just the way they are meant to be, in order for our life pattern to evolve.

Certainly it is not appropriate to say that everything is decided by fate or that everything is "meant to be." There is room for a change of plans—a margin of error. And believing that many things are destined is still no excuse for giving up, not trying hard or not aiming high. We must not sit back and let life merely happen to us just because we believe that things are happening as they should be. Only when we put forth our best effort can we assume that things are going as they should. Our input is still required and our participation is still necessary in order to make the most of a fateful opportunity, even though a higher power may be helping us along.

Words like "maybe" or "if only" are superfluous. Thinking about them with any degree of seriousness is fruitless. We cannot change the past—we can only work towards a better future. And the future begins NOW.

One final thought on the "if only" way of thinking: suppose for a moment you could go back and change your life. Suppose fate had taken a different turn. Think about whether you are so very sure that you would have wanted things to turn out differently, if it had required giving up something you now hold dear. Your choice of a different career might have meant fame and fortune, but not having the children you have now.

Certainly that would not have been worth it. You might think that staying in your hometown would have made you happier, instead of moving to your current location. But had you stayed, it is quite likely that you would not have the friends or love that you have now, and that does not seem like a happy trade. Think about your home—your pets—your career—your good health. It is true that some of these aspects of your life might have been better had you made a different decision. But other aspects might not have existed at all. I am quite sure this alternative is not an avenue you would find worth exploring.

What you have is very likely, in many ways, exactly what you should have and what you are meant to have. Your life is no doubt just as good as the other life you imagine you might have had. It may not be rewarding in the exact way you had imagined. But it may be richer by far in other ways. I dare say you would not be willing to give up certain happy and precious elements of your current life in order to have a different life.

As I have mentioned, life is full of the happy times as well as the not-so-happy ones. If we are fortunate, our moment arises from a very happy occasion. But ironically, in many cases our finest moment is actually born from a very negative occurrence. It is what we do with that bleakest of all periods that makes the difference. We can wallow in negativity; we can lose the will to live. Or we can begin living again with a renewed purpose and determination.

On the surface it is difficult to accept the fact that an event of great sorrow can bring forth a defining moment of tremendous satisfaction or emotional fulfillment.

Yet just such an occurrence altered the life of author and *Vanity Fair* columnist, the late Dominick Dunne. Dunne had been a producer and writer who was involved in the production of such films as *The Boys in the Band* and *The Panic in Needle Park* and television movies including *The Two Mrs. Grenvilles* and *An Inconvenient Woman*.

He fathered two sons, Griffin and Alex, and a daughter, Dominique. Dominique had a promising acting career ahead of her, having appeared in the highly popular film *Poltergeist* and in television films and many episodes of television series.

But in 1982, a tragedy occurred that forever altered Dominick Dunne's life. Shortly before his passing he shared with me how he coped with the tragedy. The lessons he felt he learned are a miraculous inspiration. He told his remarkable story in this way:

The moment that defined my life, changed my life, and shaped my destiny was the murder of the person whom I most cherished in my life, my daughter, Dominique, twenty-two, who was strangled to death on the night of October 30, 1982, by a former boyfriend, whom I and my two sons both loathed long before he killed her, long before we knew that he had a prior history of violence against women. When I went in to kiss her goodbye before they took her off the life support system, her head shaved, her neck purple, I allowed myself to experience the grief that overwhelmed me.

In the year that followed until the trial, detectives and prosecutors came into our lives. My former wife, Lenny, and I developed a deeper understanding of each other than we had when we were married. My two sons and I really listened to each other. What we all knew was that it was never going to be the same again. The trial was a nightmare, a farce. The judge, whom I will loathe until the day I die, led the jury into their ludicrous verdict, and the man who murdered my daughter served two and ½ years in prison. This was Step Two of my defining moment. I allowed myself to experience the rage and hatred that was inside me. I thought of hiring a killer to kill the killer. I had never been a clearly defined person until that moment. I had been sort of a feather in the breeze. I had only recently discovered, after a long Hollywood career that had ultimately failed, that I could write and that I could speak on television. What I whispered to Dominique the last time I saw her was, "Give me your talent." I firmly believe that it was she who led me into the many courtrooms I have sat in over the last twenty years, writing about justice.

Dominick Dunne reported on many high-profile cases since beginning his new phase of life, with the William Kennedy Smith, Menendez Brothers, O.J. Simpson, Phil Spector and Michael Skakel trials being among the most prominent.

Certainly a brutal murder of a child is something no parent should have to experience. But as heart-wrenching as it may be to accept, in the case of Dominick Dunne, I feel something had to happen to, in a sense, "save" him—to help him and to fulfill an element of destiny. It would seem Dominique paid the ultimate sacrifice to achieve this, but it is also my opinion that this was *her* destiny.

Indirectly, much good came from it. The remaining family members, which included Dominick, his former wife and their sons, gained a better relationship and understanding of one another. And on a larger scale, there is much to be considered. If the killer had gotten a longer sentence—had he gone to prison for what would have seemed the appropriate time, it might have provided momentary satisfaction for Dominick and family. But I feel there was a much higher good to be achieved, and it could only come from that revulsion at the trial results.

The ultimate good was to inspire Dominick to pursue and reflect upon justice for many, through his brilliant new writing and reporting career.

I am convinced that as Dominick suspected, it is absolutely true that Dominique worked in spirit with her father in the years following her murder. She certainly had a promising career as an actress. But her true calling may well have been as a crusader for justice—justice on a grander scale than one case, and her murder was the catalyst. And her partner through it all was her beloved father. What teamwork!

Kenny Kingston and the late actor/singer/songwriter Anthony Newley in Newley's London apartment.

Ellie Vallee and husband, crooner Rudy Vallee. Photo courtesy of Ellie Vallee.

Kenny and film star Debbie Reynolds at a celebrity book and memorabilia signing in Los Angeles.

Actress JoAnne Worley and Kenny.

What a difference a day made ✦ 45

Christine Jorgensen, Kenny Kingston and publicist Gretchen Fine at a party Kenny gave at Galeria Camille in Beverly Hills.

Actress Sally Struthers and Kenny in Sally's home following her psychic reading.

Kenny's mom Kaye and Kenny on the set of his Los Angeles television series.

Socialite Cobina Wright, internationally-famed nutritionist Gayelord Hauser and the immortal Mae West at a party in Kenny's Beverly Hills home.

Kenny and Ingleside Inn owner Mel Haber at Melvyn's Restaurant in Palm Springs.

Singer Steve Lawrence and Kenny backstage at a taping of Flip Wilson's television show.

Kenny and actress Susan Sullivan at Garry Marshall's Falcon Theatre following Susan's performance.

Co-author Valerie Porter, Kenny and Phyllis Diller in front of a painting of Bob Hope at Phyllis Diller's home.

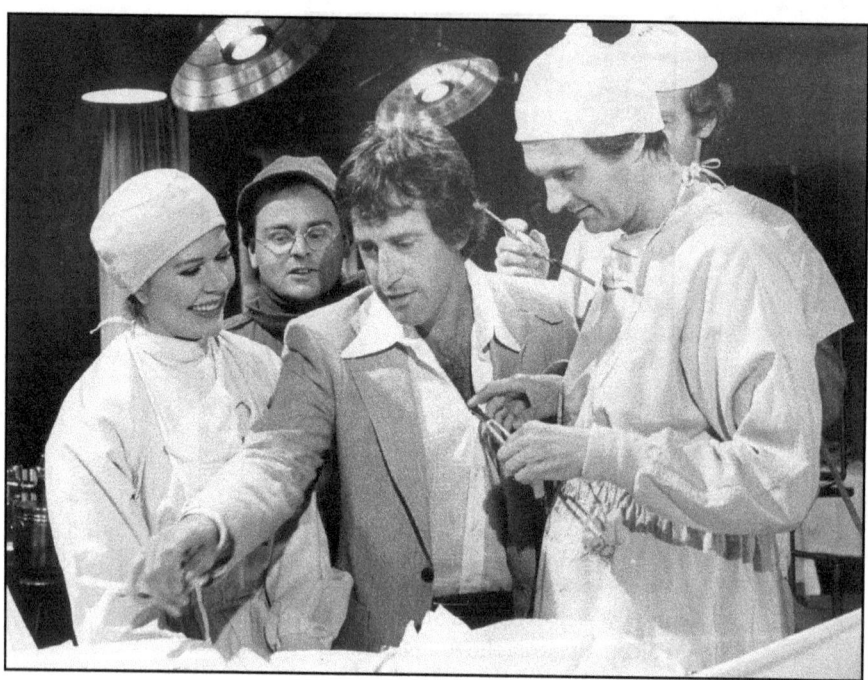

Dr. Walter Dishell in action as Technical Advisor on the set of *M*A*S*H* with cast members Loretta Swit, Gary Burghoff, Alan Alda and Mike Farrell (partially hidden). Photo courtesy of Walter Dishell, MD.

Popular U.K. astrologer Penny Thornton. Photo courtesy of Penny Thornton.

Late comic legend Flip Wilson introducing Kenny onstage at a packed opening night of Kenny's one-man show

Backstage at Italy's famed La Fenice Opera House—Kenny is giving a reading to violinist Yehudhi Menuhin

4

Stop fearing and start living

You might have automatically known what your moment was as soon as you began reading this book. If so, I hope that you have taken a little extra time to appreciate this special event and perhaps relive the feeling of accomplishment or gratitude that this moment brought you.

If you have not yet figured out what your moment was, I invite you to sit quietly somewhere that is comfortable to you, with a pad and a red felt pen (I believe that the color red brings in energy and spiritual enlightenment). Now, think back on significant times in your life. Jot them down as you recall them. There may be several times that come to mind at first. But once you have written down several of them and more or less re-lived these events in your mind, I would be very surprised if one particular event did not stand out as the most significant—the one that perhaps triggered all other events. That, Sweet Spirit, is your moment.

Now, if after doing this you still are unable to find a moment that was important to you, make sure that you are not missing out on experiencing your moment because you are not *living enough*. Living enough has nothing to do with an amount of years. It has everything to do with what effort you put into those years. Take risks—take chances—and you may be overwhelmed by the richness and sense of satisfaction that enters your life.

Take this brief test: see if you can you recall a time when you deliberately avoided an opportunity because you feared it. Ask yourself if you remember wanting very much to do something but doubting that you were capable of it.

I suspect that many people miss out on very fulfilling friendships or romances because fear prevents them from sharing their feelings. Too often, we assume people know how we feel about them. They may not.

A simple hug or even an e-mail can say, "I care." A brief phone call or greeting card that says, "I'm thinking about you" can reveal much about your feelings.

Certainly it is possible that telling someone that you feel they are special and that you value their friendship, or telling someone that they play a meaningful role in your life can be risky. Occasionally someone may not return our feelings. It is not possible to force someone to love us or even to want to be our friend.

But I dare say it is worth the risk to put our feelings on the line, considering the possible gain of a lifelong friend or potential life partner.

Sweet Spirit, think of what you may have missed out on and promise yourself right now that you will never again let fear, anxiety or self-doubt keep you from enjoying life.

Many times we have courage when it comes to protecting others or for tending to the needs of family or friends. But we must be careful that our calendar is not so full of outside commitments that we have no room left for a most precious being—ourselves!

Many years ago, when I first planned a lecture on this topic, I wondered if I would be encouraging people to be selfish. And then, I thought, "Yes, perhaps—but what's the harm in that?"

Taking care of yourself, looking out for yourself *in addition* to looking out for others is not a harmful quality. In fact, it only enhances you as a person.

Taking chances, believing in yourself enough to take a risk or do something unpopular or unconventional can be part of the true joy of living. And it is often in the process of making a bold move that we experience our best and finest moment.

"But suppose I fail?" a small voice inside may question shakily. Suppose you do? If that is the worst thing that happens in your life you will still have much to be thankful for. If down deep in your heart you know that you tried, and that no matter what, you put your best foot forward, then you will never regret that you were too frightened to make an attempt at achieving something great.

Dear One, take care not to expect failure going into a project. If you expect to fail it indicates that you lack trust in yourself or your situation. This starts you out on the wrong foot. You are going in to the venture with a negative attitude instead of expecting success and expecting a positive outcome.

Sometimes what we consider to be a failure can be our best motivator. We try harder the next time; we overcome greater obstacles in an effort to prove to ourselves that we can succeed after all. We set out to prove that what we perceived as our failure was just a "fluke"—just a one-time event that need never happen again.

Anyone who has seen a sporting event knows the determination an athlete puts into rebounding from a mistake: a basketball player jumps a little higher to make the basket, a football player runs farther towards the goal post, an ice skater lands with greater strength after a jump.

We can do this in our own lives, in our own way. It all begins with eliminating fear from our vocabulary. Find a pen and paper and write the word F-E-A-R. Now, scratch it out. The word no longer belongs to you. Below it, write a word which is its opposite and which will now replace it—F-A-I-T-H.

Have faith in life, faith in love, faith in all that is good and possible and most importantly, faith in yourself.

According to *How They Met* (Black Dog & Leventhal Publishers 2003), if not for believing in himself a young man might have cheated the world out of countless musical treasures. In April of 1965 a struggling lyricist named Tim Rice heard that another young musical talent, Andrew Lloyd Webber, was looking for what he called a "with it" writer of lyrics to collaborate on songs. Rice fancied himself to be just that person and told Lloyd Webber so in a letter he wrote to him. This eventually led to a personal meeting and to a musical partnership that skyrocketed two careers to superstardom and gave audiences such phenomenal hit shows as *Jesus Christ Superstar*, *Evita*, and *Joseph and the Amazing Technicolor Dreamcoat*.

Now it is true that both men are talented and might have been just fine without one another. Certainly, they have since gone on to work separately and create hugely successful shows on their own (Lloyd Webber has composed such hits as *The Phantom of the Opera*, *Sunset Boulevard* and *Cats* while Rice has written lyrics for *Aida* and *The Lion King*). But if Rice had not written to Lloyd Webber, perhaps the success each experienced individually would have been on a much lesser scale. Or many years might have passed before either one achieved even a share of the success they attained together. Then again, if Rice had given in to fear or doubt and talked himself out of writing the letter, Lloyd Webber might have gotten another partner. And Rice might forever have said, "That could have been me!"

What exactly is fear? Are there times when it's ok to feel afraid?

Certainly when there is a terrible storm in your city and you are concerned about your own safety or that of a loved one while driving, for example, it is only natural to feel a bit of apprehension.

If we have a dear friend or loved one in the hospital, we are bound to be concerned or anxious, thinking, "Will they recover quickly and fully?"

Sometimes even a supposedly fun activity such as going on a ride at an amusement park or trying a new sport such as skiing can cause butterflies in our stomach.

In the midst of such a tense situation it is not always easy to be rational. If only we could be, we would realize that in most cases, whether we are a child or adult, our fears are imaginary; they never materialize. We fear the unknown and our active imagination creates an outcome far worse that what actually occurs. We fear things that never happen. Think back to times in your life when you may have been guilty of this.

You may have been invited to a party but feared no one would talk to you. You may have thought that everyone else would have a good time and you would be left by yourself. In another case, you might have been worried about renewing your driver's license and imagined that you would fail the written test. Perhaps you started a new job and were convinced you would be fired the first week.

But be honest with yourself. Nine times out of ten, you went to the party and had a wonderful time, maybe even made a new friend or two. You passed the written test with flying colors. And now, several years later, you are still employed by the company you were positive would fire you.

Regardless of your religion, I think you will find comfort from the philosophy of St. Frances de Salles regarding fear: *"The same everlasting Father who cares for you today will care for you tomorrow and every day. Either He will shield you from suffering or give you unfailing strength to bear it. Be at peace, then, and put aside all anxious thoughts and imaginations."*

I have counseled people who tell me they have a great fear of going before the public to give a presentation at a business meeting or to introduce the day's speaker at a charity luncheon. They tell me they definitely are not imagining their fear—it is real to them.

For anyone who has ever suffered from anxiety before giving a performance of any kind, take note. Glamorous singer and actress Michele Lee has done it all. She has appeared in the Broadway and film versions of *How to Succeed in Business Without Really Trying* and in other films such as *The Love Bug* and *Along Came Polly*. She has worked extensively in films-for-television and audiences remember her from her long-running stint on *Knot's Landing*. This multi-talented lady has an exciting moment to share pertaining to overcoming fear. Her moment included interactions with a mind-boggling array of famous names from the world of theatre and it reflects a true triumph:

> *In 1973 I was asked to replace the lead in the Broadway musical "Seesaw" during its out-of-town tryouts.*
>
> *During the course of the play's run in Detroit as the original actress continued her performance on stage every evening, I rehearsed with Ken Howard and a very young, very tall and very green Tommy Tune who was also joining the cast.*
>
> *I was memorizing the play as it was being rewritten. I was learning the choreography as it was being restaged. Cy Coleman and Dorothy Fields were teaching me their songs as they were deciding which ones were never going to make it to opening night.*
>
> *Opening night. In just two weeks.*
>
> *I took a huge chance and I realized at that moment in my life I could do anything I wanted to do. We all can.*

This philosophy really says it all. I feel motivated by Michele's experience and am sure you do, too. Psychically, I feel her butterflies in her tummy were the inspiration and anticipation of Michele's future success. It would have been easy for her to back out of the show or not accept the role to begin with on such short notice.

To some people, their motto is, "When in doubt do nothing." But that philosophy, while it sounds good on the surface, might be just a cover up for laziness or fear. Instead of giving in to her fear, Michele used it, conquered it and was made a better person for having done so. And I am certain that the countless audiences who have enjoyed her performances through the years are thrilled that she persevered.

It is healthy to feel a certain amount of tension. Performers go through it all the time. Through my mother, I met her friend, the original First Lady of the American Theater, Katharine Cornell. I was a child when I became acquainted with "Miss Kit" as I called her. I once asked her if she ever felt fear before appearing in a play. "Oh, if Miss Kit didn't have butterflies she'd never want to go before an audience again!" she responded with a gracious smile.

She explained that it was the adrenaline that kept her alert, kept her senses aware and allowed her to give her best performances. "No matter what work you do, when you stop feeling flutters of excitement—that slight sense of danger when doing something important—then don't do it. Find something new," she told me. "Every night should feel a little bit like opening night."

To this day, I am happy to say that I still feel the faint nervous energy before doing a lecture or appearing or radio or television, and I know Miss Kit is pleased.

If you are taking on a new task, beginning a new relationship, opening your own business for the first time, it is only natural to feel uncertain. But remember that it is sometimes only by taking a risk that we are able to accomplish something truly great. Imagine the satisfaction in turning what once seemed like an almost impossible task into a success.

It is so easy to say, "I can't do this." And once you give in to that feeling it is even easier to feel the same way the next time something challenging comes along. So, in the same way that you removed "fear" from your vocabulary, I invite you to do the same with "can't."

And while you are removing words, "impossible" is another negative word that you can do without. What seems impossible may in reality only be a bit more difficult. It may simply take a bit longer to achieve a goal but it is still within your reach as long as you visualize it there and do not allow yourself to be overcome with fear, anxiety or self-doubt.

Fear, anxiety, stress or depression can all be stumbling blocks that keep us from achieving a goal or reaching our moment—the pinnacle of our life. Yet mastering these negative emotions can be a great motivator. Imagine the strength and confidence that can be derived from taking charge of your stress, overcoming your fear and overruling your anxiety or depression. We have only to re-read Michele Lee's moment to see what a turning point the mastery of fear or stress can be.

I personally feel the concept of stress is overrated. If stress killed as many people as we may have been led to believe, it would be impossible to walk the boulevard, because bodies would be strewn everywhere!

There is good stress and bad stress. True, losing a job, getting a divorce, raising a family can play havoc with one's nerves. But it can also get the blood pumping, the adrenaline flowing. It can give us the extra energy needed to complete a task or do something that might rationally seem too difficult.

Use that adrenaline, Sweet Spirit! Make it work for you, not against you. Defy your stress. Under no circumstances should you give in to it.

Here is some advice I give to clients who say they desperately need time away, but cannot afford to take a vacation for financial or time-related reasons: Take a brief "time out," a "mini vacation," every day.

This is your time to rest, to re-charge your personal batteries. You can certainly find an hour or two, or even just twenty minutes, to claim as your own. Read a book, take a walk, watch television. Indulge in a long bath or shower—anything that gives you pleasure.

Put your problems on hold for this brief time and you will be better refreshed and more able to cope with your problems when you return. You may even find that they were not as bad as you thought they were.

Eventually, advance from a few minutes or a couple of hours to a whole day to yourself. There's Mother's Day, Father's Day; there is no reason you cannot invent a new holiday and title it My Day. Go to a movie, go for a drive.

Most importantly, do not feel guilty. You will be better able to cope with your world if you are a more relaxed, refreshed person. You will be more capable of helping those around you if you have taken time to help yourself first. There is no sin in putting aside your problems for a brief period of time. They will still be there if you choose to find them again.

I have a plaque next to my bed that gives me great comfort each night before I retire. It says, "Before going to bed at night, give your problems to God. He's up all night anyway." This is so thought-provoking, and it brings me great happiness.

I have been blessed with a relatively happy, upbeat attitude my whole life. My feeling is that depression is a luxury very few can afford. I feel that we cannot afford to wallow in sadness for too long because it stands in the way of some wonderful experiences that await us. We can choose to be happy or sad—so why be sad?

The animal world, too, has stories of overcoming obstacles and surviving against seemingly impossible odds. I live in a home that is perched on a hill. To make the most of the view, on the back side of the property there are many windows and sheets of glass overlooking the hills and city lights. This is delightful for me. Occasionally it is not so good for feathered visitors to the property.

One summer day I heard a "crack" against one of the windows. I looked out to see a little brown morning dove lying dazed on the pavement about a foot from one of the windows. It had obviously hit the glass hard and seemed to be struggling just to stay conscious. Valerie and I were working on a previous book project and took time out to watch the poor thing. "I don't know what to do for it," Valerie sighed. "Let's send it healing energy," I suggested, and we did.

More than an hour later, the little bird had moved slightly and seemed to be able to take a few wobbly steps. After another hour it was even more improved but clearly unable to fly, since Valerie went out to the patio and it seemed frightened of her nearness but never made an effort to fly away.

She put birdseed and water near it and constructed a makeshift "cage" with patio chairs so that the creature might feel a bit more protected from us.

We again sent healing thoughts as night came upon us, and I confess we had concerns whether the small bird would survive till morning, though we were not about to give up hope.

Come morning, it was still there, weak but more alert. It ate some of the birdseed, which was a good sign. Amazingly, the bird stayed in the back patio for another day and eventually Valerie removed the "cage" of chairs. It walked around a bit, covering more ground, and we were encouraged.

The following morning I heard Valerie cry out, "Oh, no!" as she walked out by the pool. I looked in the water and there was the poor little dove, floating face up, his little eyes shining. I joined Valerie, but said, "It seems to be moving just a little!" We got the pool net and as I began scooping it out, I swear the bird looked me right in the eyes, like it knew I was trying to help! I drained water away from it as I held it in the net. Sure enough, when I gently placed the bird on the decking around the pool, it shook, sputtered, fell over, got up again…and lived! We immediately named our little friend "Lucky," because it certainly had been just that so far.

Lucky lived with us a few more days, rather coming to like its new "home," I believe. But we feared it might never learn to fly again if it became too comfortable. This was dangerous because of cats, raccoons and other animals in the neighborhood that visit the property from time to time. When the pool man visited, I told him of my concern. Before I could express an approval or disapproval of his technique, he said, "I can make Lucky fly" and he walked quickly toward the little bird, as though shooing it away.

This was not the method I would have used, but sure enough, Lucky flapped his wings quickly and flew to the top of the wrought iron fence. A moment later, he flew off into the sky.

A couple of days later a bird that looked very much like Lucky came back to our patio, this time with a feathered friend. We gave them both birdseed and water and they lingered awhile, perhaps as Lucky explained, "These are the people who helped me when I was injured and frightened."

If a tiny bird can overcome such frightening obstacles, imagine what we as humans can do.

There are many forms of fear to conquer. Among them is fear of the spirit world. Naturally, it has never been a problem for me because I never remember a time when I did not have a belief in the Sweet Spirits, or when I did not have encounters with them.

But I realize there are people who are not familiar with this phenomenon and one such person was actress Sally Struthers. I say "was" because Sally later signed a photo to me saying, "Thank you for taking the fear out of the spirit world for me." She co-starred for many years in the hugely popular television series *All in the Family* and has appeared in many television films and on stage in *Grease* and *The Odd Couple* in recent years. She has been a strong woman in the performing arena, but had no experience with, and therefore a fear of, the spirit world. Yet Sally was curious and open to the possibility and through a mutual friend, the late agent Judy Thomas, I arranged to do a private reading with Sally to include in my book *Guide to Health and Happiness*.

The reading went well and a transcript can be found in the book. But it was what happened after the reading that had the strongest impact on Sally. I told her that her father was around her in spirit and wanted to give her a hug. "Oh, no—I love him so much, but I'd be scared!" she protested. Spirits are respectful and her father chose not to press the issue of giving the hug at the moment, even though he did bring forth guidance and advice for his beloved daughter.

When the reading was completed, she telephoned her mom to share information and messages she had been given. She was engrossed in her conversation and oblivious to anyone else in the room, as she paced around the kitchen. "Mom," she said, "Kenny said Daddy was here and wanted to touch me!" Her mother told Sally how she would love to have that opportunity and gently chastised her daughter for being apprehensive.

"Well, I guess so…" Sally began. "Just a minute," she said, reaching her hand up to her shoulder as though patting something. She then became aware of her surroundings—she had walked behind the table and was up against the wall. She screamed, "Kenny—I thought you were patting me on the shoulder! I felt it! But there's no one behind me! I'm between the table and the wall!"

"Honey, you're wrong to say no one is behind you," I gently explained to her. "It's your daddy and he just felt he had to touch you since you were talking to your mom and he wanted so badly to make his presence known!"

Sally got tears in her eyes and said to her mom, who had been listening to the whole encounter over the telephone line, "Did you hear, Mom? Daddy touched me! And I wasn't afraid—I felt warm and happy! He hugged me just like it was a natural thing to do!"

Now, I am not suggesting that this was Sally's moment. But I do know because we have discussed it since then that this was a very moving and enlightening time in her life.

Releasing fear of the spirit world is a first step toward releasing the fear of death or passing, as I prefer to call it. My philosophy has always been that no one dies, they only have a "new birthday," and that's when life really begins. I believe this with all my heart. When our life on Earth is completed, our soul merely leaves the body and crosses over to the spirit world. "Death" is much too final a word. It implies the end, and to me that is not at all what happens. I believe that what happens when our time on Earth is over is that we are released to a world of unlimited possibilities, freedom from pain and access to unbelievable love and happiness. Passing into the spirit world is like walking into the next room. It is merely about taking on a slightly different form of existence. It certainly does not put an end to communication. In fact, it opens up a whole new world of possibilities.

Two of the greatest influences in my life were my grandmother Catherine Walsh Clark and my beloved mother Catherine (Kaye) Kingston. Both ladies were strong believers in the psychic world and in spiritualism, which is the idea that we can contact spirits who have passed on (which in itself is proof that the idea of the other side is nothing new that has only recently been discovered by a handful of psychics!). Surrounded by these two strong women, it seemed only natural that I would believe in spirits, even at an early age.

It is quite common to fear passing or to be uncomfortable about the topic. Often, fear of passing is based on a fear of the unknown. We wonder where we are going, what will happen to us. On Earth we become so wrapped up in physical and material things that passing away seems like a journey down an unfamiliar road (where we suspect things from our Earthly life will exist no more).

I think that perhaps the people I enjoy counseling the most are those who have lost a loved one or friend and are perhaps searching for some answers and most importantly for some comfort. How many people have said, "If only I could contact my mother once more" or "Suppose I could actually tell my father again how much I love him, or ask if he approves of my marriage?"

It is a fairly common phenomenon for someone to say, "I swear I smelled my sister's perfume last night." Many times people even say that they hear a loved one calling their name. "But is that possible?" they wonder, since the person passed away several years ago.

Sweet Spirits, my answer is that I believe with all my heart that, whether it is our spirit guides or our loved ones and friends, someone from the other side is available to us any time we truly need them, which means their love and their wisdom are within our reach. We can see, hear or feel our loved ones and benefit from their unconditional love, if we are open to it.

I have counseled people who fear passing because they have been unkind to someone on Earth. They fear they may encounter that person after they pass away, and it could be a very uncomfortable situation. By the same token, people may fear encountering someone who was terribly unkind to them. They wonder, "Will there be hatred? Will there be a fight? Must I endure the pain all over again?" Let me reassure you that there is no hatred on the other side, Sweet Spirit. Enemies may not become best friends—I would never pretend to you that this is the case. But do not fear a "showdown" in the spirit world. It need never happen unless both parties choose to resolve the turmoil from Earthly life.

I was speaking to a friend of mine, noted physician Dr. Walter Dishell. He is a medical advisor for many television series and I wanted to include his moment in this book. You will read his story later on, but first there is a related story to share. I told Dr. Dishell that one element of the book would pertain to moments that eliminate fear from our lives. "Would eliminating fear of death count?" he asked. He then proceeded to share a moment that his mother Toddy had experienced, which was really a glimpse of the other side just shortly before she passed.

He told me that his mom called the experience a dream. I told him, after hearing it, that I prefer to believe she actually visited the spirit world briefly for a preview of the world she would soon be a part of. "Well, whatever it was, Kenny," he smiled, "it took the fear out of death for my mom and for her family." He wrote the details of his mom's experience as he recalls her telling it to her family, and I offer the story to you here:

Toddy's Dream

I had the most wonderful dream, darlings. I dreamt that I was in a huge green field, much like that of Maria in The Sound of Music. *It was a beautiful sun-filled day with the bluest of skies, not a cloud to be seen. I was slowly walking and the wind was lightly blowing through my hair. I could see several people in the distance and as I came upon them I realized that I knew them. The first person I saw was my sweet little Mama and not far behind of course was Papa. I could see a young man coming towards me...my beloved husband, Bobby. I was so happy.*

He held my hand as we continued to walk through the field. Suddenly, I noticed all the beautiful flowers that were blooming as well as the bees and butterflies that so happily danced around them. I heard my name being called and turned slightly to see my sister Rose and then my brother Ephraim. They joined us as we continued to now dance through the field. We soon came upon our baby sister, Lillian. Oh what a glorious moment we all had, giggling together. It was just like old times. Our laughter and excitement was so intense...and just then I opened my eyes and looked around to see that I was in my bed, in my bedroom with the caretaker near my side and smiling down at me.

When I realized that I had been dreaming, I started to cry. Then I quickly closed my eyes and tried to go back to the field. I was so sad that I had returned to my life as it were...oh to be in that field once more with my family. I so wanted to join them. I felt them calling to me. I asked my daughter-in-law, who do you think will be the first of my family that I will see when I go? She was certain it would be Bobby, then Mama and Papa, Ephraim, Rose and Lillian. "Really?" I asked. "Oh yes," she replied. With my eyes closed I could feel the smile on my face.

I couldn't wait to go to sleep each night, hoping that I would be joining them in the meadow once again.

This beautiful story was told to the Dishell family by Toddy Dishell, age 96, two weeks prior to her passing.

One last fear people have is the fear of being alone or lonely. But if we cultivate hobbies or interests—anything from sports to painting to simply reading or enjoying music—we need not be lonely, for we have stimulating activities in our lives. And there are certainly times when we are our own best company.

Besides, Dear Ones, in my opinion we are never alone, for we have our loved ones in spirit around us. Talk to the spirit of your mother, your father, your husband or wife. Tell them you miss them, ask them to visit you or send you a signal that they are around you. You may not immediately see them, feel them or hear them. But they may contact you in subtle ways, so stay alert. Gentle reminders of their presence may come in the form of their favorite song playing on the radio or television when you are thinking of them. You may see a license plate with their name on it, or find a flower or feather…something that may on the surface seem ordinary. Perhaps this might be considered a coincidence. And then again, it may well be a sign of tender love that your loved one has taken great pains to send to you from the other side.

And of course, if you have a belief in a higher force, whether you call that power God or Jesus or Buddha or Moses, you know that this is a power you can call upon at any time for comfort. When I was young, a neighbor of mine was novelist Taylor Caldwell. I know she shared a belief in the spirit world and had a strong sense of spirituality. I came across a quote of hers on a page of a calendar (*Hugs for Everyone, 2004*) and it brought back fond memories of this delightful lady. It seems like a fitting way to close this chapter:

> *I am not alone at all, I thought. I was never alone at all. And that, of course is the message. We are never alone. Not when the night is darkest, the wind coldest, the word seemingly most indifferent. For this is still the time God chooses.*

5

Learn from the past; live in the future

To quote a wise saying, "The past is the past and the charm of the past is that it is the past."

I have always appreciated this statement for its simplicity and honesty. Good or bad, what is in our past—whether it is something that happened last year, last week or just last night—becomes a part of our personal history along life's journey.

Naturally, we are unable to change past events but we can use what happened during those events, and what we learned from them, to improve upon our future. In many cases, a brief nostalgic look back at people or events from the past is well worthwhile. Fond memories of happy times or beloved people can be very enjoyable. And, in fact, what we are learning as we search for our moment is that it often requires a look back in order to then go forward as a better person.

However, dwelling on the past, even if it was wonderful, limits our progress because we should instead be working toward a new and even better tomorrow.

Why rest on our laurels when there is more success for us—more happiness—if we are open to it? If you have accomplished one goal, start on the next. In fact, I am a firm believer in jotting down our goals so that we can have the sense of accomplishment that comes with crossing them off when we achieve them. Not every goal need be monumental. Set a few small goals along the way purely for the satisfaction of knowing you can quickly achieve them.

Even a daily "to do" list is a form of setting small goals. And we all know the satisfaction that mastering that list can provide. It is a real morale booster.

My dear friend Mae West refused to rest on her laurels or let disappointment take root in her mind. She always had her next project in sight.

She was eighty-five years old when she completed what was to be her last film, *Sextette*.

At the conclusion of filming there was a studio screening. The audience did not receive the film well. Instead of the success that Mae had imagined, there was a heavy silence in the screening room, perhaps because in the film Mae played a twenty-eight-year-old bride who was desired and loved by men everywhere (Timothy Dalton, Regis Philbin, Rex Reed and Ringo Starr all played roles in the film).

Mae, always the optimist, left the screening with her companion, director/writer/ producer Herbert Kenwith. They slid into her limo and sat deep in thought for a brief moment, each gazing out their respective windows.

And then Mae said to Kenwith, "Well, dear, that was yesterday. I've got to think about tomorrow."

The comment was heavy with meaning. She had reflected on the conclusion of the project for a moment, honoring its importance but also realizing, perhaps, that she could improve upon her work the next time around. And then she decided to leap right into looking forward to new horizons. Even though *Sextette* was Mae's last film, I know from our telephone conversations and from visiting her in her apartment in Hollywood's Ravenswood building, that she was planning new projects, which sadly went uncompleted when she passed away.

Even if you have achieved something wonderful, to sit back and assume that this is the best you could do is to short-change yourself. What you consider to be your greatest accomplishment may only be the tip of the iceberg; but you will never know if you stop challenging yourself to do more. You will never know what new memories—what delightfully happy moments—might lie ahead unless you put your past in its rightful place and move on.

Even more important than setting aside a happy occurrence is the need to release negative people or situations from your past. No matter what happened previously, the key is to release the negativity instead of clinging to it and re-living it or worse yet, expecting it to be the normal pattern of your future.

This is not an easy task, certainly. Some people or events are very evil and painful. But if we can begin to visualize a door closing on those situations, we can see a new one opening.

I always tell my clients that we can choose to be happy or sad, so why be sad? Why wallow in our misery when we can use our pain or hurt to make us even stronger than we thought possible?

Each day is a fresh start. Every morning separates us from the morning before and brings a new opportunity our way. We have a clean slate for that day and are free to make new, positive choices, whether large or small.

It is a common practice to think of New Year's Day as a fresh start, but there is no reason the fresh start must be limited to January 1st. We need not be dictated to by a calendar but instead by our mind and heart.

I was fortunate to receive a request to give a private reading to famed novelist and playwright W. Somerset Maugham on the occasion of his eightieth birthday.

What impressed me the most about this delightfully talented man was that he exuded such a positive attitude. A negative person might have thought, "I'm eighty years old—why have a psychic reading about my future—what's left to know?" Another negative person might have thought, "There's been so much wrong in my life that I guess that's just what I'm supposed to experience. Why get a psychic reading to find out what I already know?"

But Mr. Maugham was upbeat—as excited about life as a thirty-year-old might be. I asked him what his secret to longevity was thus far and he said, "Kenny, I've never carried the burden of memories like a suitcase on my back."

What a profound statement! It was evident from our conversation that this was a man who had clearly decided to be happy. He had decided not to let his past have control over his future. He had chosen to be a survivor and to create his own happiness by not allowing negativity to take root.

Maugham was a prolific writer of such literary works as *Of Human Bondage*, *The Razor's Edge* and *The Letter*. Some ninety-eight films were made from his material during his lifetime. I credit his positive attitude with his success, coupled, of course, with a tremendous talent.

It would be easy to say that he was a successful writer and therefore had little to be unhappy about. But we all have our share of disappointments or unpleasant events. It is what we do with them that determines the level of happiness, contentment and success we will enjoy. The key is not to show that we have problems, to not let them become a dominant force in our life. We must not let our problems define who we are.

We may think that our problems are unique or that we are the only ones suffering. But, of course, that is not true.

In order to move on from unhappiness and release the negativity of the past, we must be prepared to forgive, at least to the point that we can forget. Depending upon what the negativity was, it may involve forgiving a stranger, a loved one, a spouse, a co-worker or even ourselves.

Forgiving in no way means that we approve of what was done to us or what caused our pain, or that we would ever accept the same treatment in the future. But it is necessary to come to some degree of understanding and acceptance of the person or circumstances that helped lead to our unhappiness so that we can avoid the same problem or emotions in the future. This sense of forgiveness may be one of the hardest things you will ever do.

The forgiveness I am talking about involves giving up the right to forever assume the position of "victim." To let a negative experience ruin our lives is to let the person or circumstances that harmed you have power over you.

If you were abused or harmed mentally, physically or emotionally, you will need every ounce of strength to overcome that abuse or harm so that it does not destroy your life. Even if the harm done to you was quite intense, you have the power within to take charge of it.

If it was a person who harmed you, what better way to show them that they have no power over you? As the saying goes, "Success is the best revenge." The statement takes a somewhat lighthearted approach to a serious emotion. The word "revenge" in general has (and rightfully so) a negative connotation. Seeking revenge or a way to extract your own form of justice can cause as much harm for you because of the vicious emotions it stirs as it would ever cause for the person you seek revenge upon.

Blame a situation or person for a brief time but not for a lifetime. Certainly the anger or hurt is strong at first. But we only nurture and feed it if we dwell on it.

I once had a client whose son was murdered when he was a young boy. A man kidnapped the child and then intentionally pushed him into a lake and the boy drowned. The man was eventually caught and sentenced to life in prison.

Many years later, when the mother first started seeing me as a client, she told me she still suffered not only grief but extreme anger. Each time she visited her son's grave to leave flowers, she told me she prayed that his killer would also pass away. Most of her waking hours, she told me, were spent wishing evil for the murderer.

I saw her several times for private counseling and one time she sat down at my reading table and said, "A strange thing happened. The murderer passed away in prison yesterday. I thought this would make me very happy and put an end to the whole tragedy. But it hasn't helped."

She told me that she realized that nothing would bring back her beloved son and that gloating over someone else's passing certainly was not something she would have wanted her son to learn from her.

I was able to contact her son in spirit, which by then was possible because quite some time had passed and he was adjusted to the other side. It takes some souls a long time to recover from a violent passing.

We asked her son if he was happy the prisoner had passed away and what else would make him happy. He said nothing about the prisoner but said that what would really make him happy was to see his mother happy. "He's telling me about candy," I told her. "Is there something about a candy store?"

Tears glistened in her eyes. "He always told me that he wanted to own a candy store when he grew up," she whispered.

"Is it possible for you to do this, in his memory?" I asked.

"Well, I've been thinking of changing careers," she said tentatively, "if it would really make him happy I could do it."

To sum it up, I saw her again a few months later and she was an entirely different person, genuinely smiling for the first time. She opened a candy store, as her son had wanted to do.

"Each time I see a child come into my store, hand out a piece of candy and see the child smile, I think of my son. I'm living the dream he wanted to live and I realize that this is the best ending to our tragedy," she said.

The pain may always be there for her on some level, but I also know that it has been lessened considerably.

Before we move away from the topic of forgiveness, it is worth mentioning the one person we may have the hardest time forgiving—ourself.

Countless times I have counseled people who tell me they are sure that they could achieve more in life if they weighed less, were prettier, or if they did not abuse drugs or alcohol. In each case, if we truly believe a supposed flaw is holding us back, we can change it. We can lose weight, get a makeover, or stop abusing drugs or alcohol.

But instead, too many times I hear, "My whole family's overweight, so what can I do about it?" "My father was an alcoholic, that's why I drink too much." If someone abuses a child, their defense is that *they* were abused as a child. How easy it is to say, "I can't help it—it's meant to be."

Sweet Spirits—take responsibility for your actions! Break a negative pattern instead of assuming you have to accept and continue it. If you have been rejected by someone in business or your personal life, it does not always follow that rejection will become a permanent part of your life.

Believe instead that the rejection came because something or someone better is just around the corner.

I invite you to adapt a philosophy that I believe in. It says that "every knock is a boost." In other words, turn your temporary letdown into a motivation to achieve something even better. Become a survivor.

If the path you have grown comfortable with is no longer appealing to you, dare to try something new. One person who did this is Mel Haber. He is the owner of the enchanting, exclusive and highly successful Ingleside Inn, long a haven for celebrities and others who enjoy a little piece of tranquility just off the main street in beautiful Palm Springs, California. Some of the stars who have stayed at the Inn or dined in gourmet class Melvyn's Restaurant include Howard Hughes, Bob Hope, Jerry Lewis, Cher, Frank Sinatra, Liza Minnelli, Diahann Carroll, John Travolta—truly a "Who's Who" of show business names.

Establishing the Ingleside Inn as the resort that it is today took a huge leap of faith on the part of Mel Haber, as he explains:

> *One of the most defining moments in my life took place in 1975. I made a decision to abandon a successful career as a manufacturer in New York and move to Palm Springs, California. In hindsight I was going through the proverbial "mid-life crisis."*
>
> *Not only was I changing my place of residence but I decided to go into the hotel and restaurant business, rationalizing that if I was able to just grind out a living in this desert paradise I would be a happy camper. So, I moved to a town where I knew nobody and nobody knew me, went into a business I knew absolutely nothing about and left an industry where over twenty-three years I had become well known and successful. None of this made any sense.*
>
> *However, there is a cliché that God watches over "drunks and children." You can add Mel Haber to that. Over the next thirty years I became a "big fish in a little pond" and had the opportunity to meet many wonderful people in addition to some of the most famous and accomplished people in the world. In retrospect, knowing what I know now, I realize that I had no chance to succeed! I am not sure what the moral of my story is except that in certain instances your gut instinct is as good as any logical reasoning.*

Mel's moment involved closing a door on his past and taking an incredible risk on the future. It is true that he could have failed in his venture. But he would never have known if he had never tried. Look at the joy that he has taken in developing the Inn. I have stayed and dined there and can vouch for the joy Mel has brought to the countless guests the Inn has entertained.

Not only did Mel find happiness by closing one door and opening another, he chose not to worry about what others might have thought of his plan. He has become, in my opinion, one of the most respected and revered businessmen in Palm Springs and his Inn is known and loved by all.

On that subject, but from an entirely different aspect of life, is a beautifully philosophical saying that the pastor of my church shared with us one Sunday. It was apparently seen hanging on the wall of Mother Teresa's orphanage in Calcutta, India, and is rumored to have been written by her:

> *People are often unreasonable, illogical and self-centered.*
> **Forgive them anyway.**
>
> *If you are kind, people may accuse you of selfish, ulterior motives.*
> **Be kind anyway.**
>
> *If you are successful, you may win some false friends and some true enemies.*
> **Succeed anyway.**
>
> *If you are honest and frank, people may cheat you.*
> **Be honest and frank anyway.**
>
> *Transparency may make you vulnerable.*
> **Be transparent anyway.**
>
> *If you find serenity and happiness, others may be jealous.*
> **Be happy anyway.**
>
> *What you spend years building may be destroyed overnight.*
> **Build anyway.**
>
> *The good you do today may be forgotten tomorrow.*
> **Do good anyway.**

People who really want help may attack you if you help them.
Help them anyway.

Give the world the best you have and it may never be enough.
Give the world your best anyway.

You see, in the final analysis, it is between you and God.
It never was between you and them anyway.

As we look back on our life there may be several moments when Mother Teresa's verse has great meaning. It is far better to know that we did not allow what others thought of us in the past to affect how we approached the future.

Parting with the past always holds potential for sadness. We leave a vacation spot and wish we could have stayed longer; we take a relative to the airport and wish their visit could have been extended; we move to another city and remember wistfully the good times we had in the old location.

But unquestionably the most devastating sorrow comes when a loved one or friend passes to the spirit world. And no one, no matter how powerful, no matter how wealthy, can escape that sadness. They cannot buy their way or negotiate their way out of it. The loss is still there.

As strongly as I believe in the other side, I have still felt the overwhelming sorrow that accompanies the loss of a loved one. It is a normal emotion—a natural reaction—and in my opinion, a healthy one. The key is to put that emptiness into perspective and to somehow take control over this most painful of emotions. We must believe with all our heart that we can make peace with the loss and that in fact it is not really a loss as much as a change, which was inevitable. Change happens and perhaps the best we can do is to search for the lesson we are meant to learn from the change.

If you are fortunate enough not to have lost anyone in your life, my blessings to you and I hope it will be a long time before anyone close to you passes to the other side. But I also gently advise you to read the following pages anyway. Keep the book handy so that if an event such as this happens, you might find the tremendous peace of mind you so richly deserve. And, of course, countless people have a curiosity about the other side and want to read all they can on the subject. Some have a fear of "death," which I trust can be eased or eliminated with more insight into the reality of the spirit world.

People have seen me repeatedly on television over the years and they may have heard me on radio, always speaking about my belief in the spirit world and my communication with those spirits. They often tell me they get the impression that what I do seems not only entertaining but easy. For me, it is easy, because I enjoy it so much. But do not lose sight of the fact that I take myself and the spirit world very seriously. I am one-hundred percent convinced that the world of spirit is real because I have lived with daily examples of it in my own life. I enjoy using my spirit communications to help others. All I ask, as I ask during my lectures around the world, is that you keep an open mind and allow me an opportunity for spirit and in this case, information about spirit, to come forward.

Truly, then, far from feeling separated from our departed friends—far from feeling that no one can help or that no one is watching over us, I say instead that your loved ones are within reach. No one "dies"; they only have a new birthday. This involves birth into a new life that is filled with opportunities to be removed from sickness or pain, to be reunited with loved ones who have passed and to continue to watch over and comfort those of us still on Earth.

It is only natural to cry at the physical loss of a loved one, whether it is a relative, friend or a beloved pet. But eventually we must dry our tears, be happy for their awakening into the spiritual realm, and look forward to a beautiful reunion with them one day.

They would certainly not want us to spend the rest of our time on Earth paralyzed by grief.

I was at a dinner party in the home of a well-known celebrity couple in Beverly Hills. Guests in attendance were from all aspects of the entertainment world. Many were taking turns speaking to singers Steve Lawrence and his wife Eydie Gorme. Their son Michael had passed on not long beforehand. They were naturally distraught and told several of us that they were considering cancelling an upcoming tour of many cities.

"I think it's the right thing to do," said a very famous redheaded actress. "You need this time to cry," she said. "Just cry as much as you want… for as long as you want," she urged them. "And don't do the tour."

When she had walked away, I told Steve and Eydie that I strongly disagreed with the actress. "Cancelling the tour won't bring Michael back," I told them. "Naturally, you are in pain over his passing. But do you think he would want you to stop doing the thing that you love, knowing the joy you could give to your audiences? Why not go on with the tour and dedicate it to Michael's memory?"

"Do you really think so, Kenny?" Steve asked. "I've always believed in you," he said. Eydie said softly, "Dedicating it to Michael—that sounds lovely. But we'll just have to think about it."

I am happy to say that I read a newspaper article not long afterwards and this legendary pair of entertainers did indeed go on with their tour, dedicating it to the memory of their wonderful son. They also appeared on the Jerry Lewis Labor Day Telethon for Muscular Dystrophy and gave a check in memory of Michael. I am sure he was proud of his parents.

In the same way that our loved ones in spirit would not want us to forever grieve, they would also not want us to be bitter about their passing. I truly believe that spirits wish only the best for us and the best is not ruining our lives by turning our back on future happiness.

Debonair dancer and film star Fred Astaire brought enjoyment to fans around the world, myself included. He seemed to always have a ready smile and gentleness about him.

Then his wife Phyllis passed away. I was living in Beverly Hills at the time and saw him walking one of the boulevards some time later. He had a top coat on, the collar turned up, a hat pulled down low, as though he were shielding himself from the world. I walked into a nearby shop and the clerk said, "Did you see Fred Astaire walk by?"

I told her that I had and she said, "It's so hard to watch. He used to pass by and smile or wave, but now he not only doesn't smile, he seems angry at everyone."

I had to agree with her. By chance I saw him walking a couple of weeks later, still appearing bitter, still cut off from people. I took a chance by approaching him, not knowing what his reaction would be.

"Mr. Astaire—Fred?" I called out.

He stopped and looked at me. "Yes?" he questioned.

I introduced myself. "I know who you are, Kenny," he said, none too kindly.

I told him, "I've sat in the dark so many times and watched you. You've cheered me up as you have so many others worldwide. Perhaps it's my turn to try cheering you up ever so slightly."

He patiently listened as I told him that his wife was in a much better place and that if he would be open to her, she would come back to visit him in spirit. "You're not helping her by your attitude," I chided him. "I'm sure nothing would please her more than to see the gentle and kind husband she knew and loved return."

He thanked me as we parted ways, but I was really not sure my message had had any impact.

Several weeks later I attended a social function at the famed Cocoanut Grove nightclub at the Ambassador Hotel in Los Angeles. Low and behold, one of my fellow guests was Fred Astaire, looking slightly uncomfortable yet smiling and speaking to others in attendance.

I passed near him on my way to my table and heard, "Kenny! I want to thank you."

I came closer and he said quietly, "It was a turning point for me the moment I met you. I was forced to pull myself out of my troubles and move on in the world."

I could not have been happier for him and I know the entertainment world and audiences everywhere gained immeasurably from his return to life, so to speak. He seemed to be loving life again and I am sure he received love in return. He had learned that he could hold memories of his wife close to his heart yet also clear a space there for the making of new memories.

In fact, in his later years he found love again, marrying former jockey Robyn Smith.

6

Success

"To laugh often and love much; to win the respect of intelligent persons and the affection of children; to earn the approbation of honest citizens and endure the betrayal of false friends; to appreciate beauty; to find the best in others; to give of one's self; to leave the world a bit better, whether by a healthy child, a garden patch or a redeemed social condition; to have played and laughed with enthusiasm and sung with exultation; to know even one life has breathed easier because you have lived—this is to have succeeded."

– Ralph Waldo Emerson

This beautiful quotation from Emerson really captures the true essence of why we are all placed on Earth. It illustrates the various forms that "success" can take, whether it is the satisfaction of being a parent, a creative artist, a doctor or lawyer, or perhaps to give an animal a happy home. Our goal in life, as Emerson so eloquently points out, is to succeed on whatever level and perhaps on as many levels, as we can, so long as we give happiness and in turn, receive it.

Much of what he discusses involves laughter and joy and, of course, these should be the main goals in striving for success.

Strange though it may seem, this chapter on success came about in part due to a client of mine, reclusive and eccentric billionaire Howard Hughes.

I encountered him quite by accident in a hotel barbershop. I had arrived a bit early for a manicure and saw that my manicurist Ruth was working on a tall, slender man. Ruth called "Hello" to me and I responded not only with a "Hello" but a brief psychic message that I had just received when I heard the sound of her voice.

I saw her client glance toward me. Ruth seemed a bit flustered and said, "How do your nails look to you, Mr. Hughes?"

Hearing that, the man abruptly jumped up, tossed some bills down on her table and began a quick exit, stopping briefly in front of me.

"You're a fortuneteller?" he asked.

"Well, I'm a psychic/medium," I answered.

"May I have a business card, please?" he inquired, and I handed him one.

After he rushed out, I took my seat with Ruth. "That was such a mistake I made," she said unhappily.

"Why?" I asked.

"Don't you know who that was?" she asked. "That was Howard Hughes. He's asked me to never refer to him by name when I do his nails. And this time I forgot!"

A couple of nights later my telephone rang. When I answered, I heard, "Is this Kenny Kingston?" I said yes and he inquired, "How does one go about setting an appointment with you?"

That was the beginning of my association with Howard. The events that occurred are too many to mention here. It should be noted that he remained my client *after the time it was rumored that he was in seclusion and even after the time that it was reported that he'd passed away.* Two brief items can be revealed, however.

One time I walked Howard to his car following a reading I had given to him and I noticed that it was an old model, slightly dented and inexpensive car, certainly not the Rolls-Royce, Jaguar or Mercedes I would have expected.

"Howard—why don't you drive a more elegant car?" I smiled.

He wisely answered, "Kenny—who do I have to impress?"

Regarding this chapter, he once told me, when I was working on an idea for my first book, that he thought I should write a book about how to deal with success once you have it. "You could charge $5,000 for it," he said proudly. "Most people don't know what to do with themselves or how to handle success once they've achieved it. They'd clamor for your advice," he said.

Well, Howard—I never wrote the book about success. But I am writing a chapter about it right now, and I dedicate it to you.

It has always been my experience that if you want something done, ask a busy person to do it. It seems that people who are busy are achievers. They are motivated and energetic. They are usually successful and it is easy to see why.

One such person is actress Susan Sullivan. She has had a long and successful career, appearing in the television mini-series *Rich Man, Poor Man* and more recently in the series *Dharma and Greg*. I met her when I interviewed her for my column in *The Tolucan Times* newspaper following a performance of a play she was appearing in at Garry Marshall's Falcon Theatre in Toluca Lake, a lovely area of Southern California.

When I began work on this book, I thought of Susan and how I would like to include her comments. She was busy co-starring as "Martha" in ABC-TV's hit television show *Castle*. The show was about to be picked up for its third season. Yet she responded quickly with her moment and it reminds me of her—humorous, to the point and quite intriguing. She claimed her moment was "one of those experiences that got tattooed on my brain, forced me to wake up, change":

But first, let me say that I wasn't looking to change my ways. On the contrary, I was blissfully thinking I could stay just the same. Maybe that's always the way it is with change—we get thrown into it, kicking and screaming.

I was a ninth grader in high school and entered a contest (against tenth graders) that required memorizing a speech and delivering it on stage. Unfortunately, I won. And against tenth graders, yes, tenth graders. I must admit that it made me pretty full of myself.

The next time the contest rolled around (now I'm in the tenth grade) I again entered, but assumed I had an edge because I had won before so easily. I didn't train—no pushups or laps around the track, no endless rehearsal, in essence, no real preparation. I didn't need it; I was invincible. I didn't put in the time and energy to find something I related to personally that had my rhythm.

At the last minute, I decided to go with the Gettysburg Address. If Lincoln could make it work, so could I. Trouble is, I'm sure he must have gone over his own words many more times than I did in preparation. I went out there on the stage winging it and went up (a performer's term for forgetting one's lines) half way through. I asked if I could start again…I forgot my lines AGAIN.

Yikes, a ninth grader won. I was deeply humiliated and realized how important it is to do the work. This seems obvious, but the timing of this experience gave me an important lesson in honoring both my talent and the material. I have never been under-prepared again, whether it is for a silly little comedy or Shakespeare.

Susan's moment taught her to always be prepared. This is a valuable lesson that anyone should learn about aiming for success. It also taught her, I believe, to live each day and each moment to its fullest. Perhaps the worst thing we can do is "coast" through life, as Susan attempted to do with her second contest entry.

Even if a task seems mundane, or the event seems boring, there could be hidden magic in it. It is our challenge and responsibility to lend ourselves fully, as Susan learned, to each moment of our life. There is no excuse for gliding through the day without living up to our full potential. Certainly, it is necessary to relax, but do this by choice and at a scheduled time, not because you do not feel the task is worth your attention. Live each day fully and express gratitude for all that you are and all that you are capable of becoming.

No matter how prepared we are, though, and how much we feel we are planning our future, there is a popular expression that suggests: "Do you want to make God laugh? Tell him *your* plans."

Not only is this an amusing concept, it is also an eye-opener because it is so true. Things have a way of turning out as they are meant to. It may not be the way we want them to turn out at the time, but the events are for our ultimate good.

Whether you believe in God, Buddha or another higher force, there really is a higher plan for us, even when we think, as comedienne Phyllis Diller once did, that we are in the wrong place at the wrong time.

I have known Phyllis a long, long time. I first became aware of her when I was living in San Francisco and she was an up-and-coming comic appearing at The Purple Onion, a popular nightclub. I predicted then that she would be a tremendous success and, of course, she has had a long and illustrious career not only in stand-up but in films and television.

As she explains in her moment, some of her greatest success occurred through appearances she made with comedy legend Bob Hope. She did many USO tours with him as well as appearing in his television specials and in films with him. She has also had a wonderful career on her own, too. She shared her moment in this way and even gave it a title—Upturn at Low Tide:

> My early career took a turn for the better the night I met Bob Hope in Washington, D.C. Bob had come to the capitol to "visit his money." He noted new comic Phyllis Diller playing at the Lotus Club. He

gathered together his group of cronies (including Ben Gimbel) and brought them to see me.

The Lotus Club, a basement operation featuring Oriental food, six show girls who also "mingled," me, and the star of the revue, an attractive lesbian billed as the Irish Senorita, who wore white cotton pants in 1959, on stage.

My booking was for ten days and after each tortuous night, I'd return to the hotel a broken woman, and wonder if I could face this job to complete the run.

You see, I was at the wrong place at the wrong time. Here I am playing to sleazy traveling men and hookers, doing my innocent little comedy about home-life, children, dogs, neighbors, cops, food, etc. They aren't interested.

I follow the opening act, which is the six sluts who come out with deep décolletage, bow and leave.

I come out and bomb. My act goes straight into the toilet. It is awful. I am dying.

I had been told Bob Hope is in the audience. This makes it even worse. I'm not only bombing, I am nervous and embarrassed.

At the end of my turn I try to sneak out behind pillars to escape a confrontation, and Bob jumps up, stops me and says, "You are just great."

This, coming from my lifetime idol, made the birds sing and the sunshine come out.

Phyllis surely realized then that indeed she was exactly where she was meant to be that night; otherwise her meeting with Bob Hope might never have happened. She was booked at the Lotus Club for a reason. Playing at the club was certainly not what she had hoped for, but it was a means to an end. It was a way to help her achieve a higher goal.

Had she taken matters into her own hands and backed out of the engagement, thinking that this was the appropriate move on the path to success, she would have interfered with what was planned for her.

Naturally, we need to help ourselves. We need to work as hard as we can to become a success, instead of thinking success will find us if it is meant to. But at the same time, if we feel we have done all we can to change a circumstance, thinking we are doing the right thing to achieve a goal, consider the possibility that what we interpret as an unpleasant situation is exactly what is best for us at the moment—a stepping stone toward our real destiny.

So in fact, most success is based on being in the right place at the right time and learning to identify the fact that the "right place" may not be what we think it is.

Certainly, luck is often involved when things turn out in our favor. But hard work plays a much stronger role. And perhaps luck is mostly about recognizing opportunities and capitalizing on them.

One last thing regarding Phyllis's success: While she is known for her comedy, less known is the fact that she is an accomplished concert pianist and also a gifted artist. One of her paintings hangs in my home and a visit to her home would not be complete without seeing the vast number of creative and colorful paintings she has created.

Not content with one field of expertise, she has expanded her horizons and allowed her many gifts to have full expression.

Phyllis had a relatively late start with her comedy career, having married and begun raising children before, in her late 30s, embarking on stand-up comedy.

For her, finding her true calling took awhile. For others, they know at a tender age what their life's work should be.

Certainly it is common for a child of five or six to boast that he or she wants to grow up to be a police officer, nurse, firefighter or vet, only to change their mind the next year.

Everything is dramatic to a youngster. Their first love as a teenager is their soul mate—there could never be anyone else for them. Occasionally that may be true, but more often it is merely the first awakening to the many possibilities for love that await them as life unfolds.

However, some young people, perhaps in their teens, begin to feel truly passionate about a person or a career and it indeed molds their life and shapes their success.

A doctor friend of mine decided at seventeen not only that he would enter the medical field, but that becoming a highly compassionate doctor would be his ultimate goal.

As often happens, his happiest moment was born from pain and unhappiness. The success he has since achieved has hopefully more than compensated for the earlier tragedy for my friend Dr. Walter David Dishell. I briefly mentioned Dr. Dishell earlier when discussing his mother. Dr. Dishell is one of the country's top plastic and reconstructive surgeons who also does head and neck surgery.

I call him "David" when we speak to one another, because it is one of my favorite names since I was psychic to the Duke and Duchess of Windsor. The Duke (former King Edward VIII of England) gave up the throne for Wallis Simpson, the "woman he loved." When I gave them psychic readings, I referred to him by his given name, David.

Back to Dr. Dishell: in addition to his thriving medical practice, he has been medical advisor to many classic television shows, including *M*A*S*H*, *Trapper John* and *Medical Center* among many others. He has authored several medically-themed scripts in his busy career and has been a medical reporter/producer on many news programs.

As he explains, the event that changed his life occurred when he suffered an injury and spent weeks recuperating:

> *I was seventeen years old and it was a week before my high-school graduation and senior prom. As was the custom, the senior class ditched school and went to a local lake where we held our senior picnic. While horsing around with four of my friends, they each grabbed one of my limbs and decided to throw me into the water.*
>
> *Unfortunately, only three let go at the same time. The fourth friend continued to hold onto my right leg as my body flipped over. I severely twisted my knee and was in excruciating pain. One week later, instead of going to my prom and attending graduation, I was in the hospital undergoing knee surgery.*
>
> *While lying in pain in the hospital after surgery, I confided to my mother that the doctors and nurses that were taking care of me were fairly insensitive to my pain and suffering. They weren't very nurturing or sympathetic to my situation. After all, I not only had to have surgery and was in pain, but on top of that, I had to miss my senior prom (I had a very hot date) and my graduation (with honors) as well*
>
> *I told my mother that, "when I become a doctor, I'm going to be more sensitive and caring with my patients than these doctors were." The incident at my senior picnic is the event that made me decide to enroll in the pre-med program at the University of Michigan and become a doctor. That decision has influenced the course of my entire life.*

It is clear that for Dr. Dishell, his path to success began at seventeen. For Phyllis Diller, it was many years later. This should be encouraging to both younger and older readers. Perhaps you are young and wondering if the moment you have in mind really is your turning point. As you can see from past examples, Harry Truman met Bess at the tender age of six. Dr. Walter Dishell was a teenager when his life changed.

On the other hand, if you're in your 30s, 40s or beyond and do not feel that you have encountered a life-changing moment yet, take heart from Phyllis Diller and others (Beverly Garland, for example) whose moment occurred slightly later in life. Perhaps your moment is yet to occur and that should be a very exciting thought and certainly something to look forward to.

Not every moment is Earth-shattering in its importance, meant to skyrocket you to greatness. Greatness is a relative term. Helen Keller was born blind, deaf and mute. She overcame those obstacles to become a public figure with much to offer in the way of inspiration. Her life story and association with her teacher Annie Sullivan was the basis for the film *The Miracle Worker* starring Patty Duke and Annie Bancroft.

Helen Keller's words are poignant and powerful:

> *I long to accomplish a great and noble task, but it is my chief duty to accomplish humble tasks as though they were great and noble.*

In her case, the humble tasks she accomplished were indeed also noble and great because of the effort she had to exert in order to achieve simple things that we who have the power of sight, hearing and speech take for granted. She became an example and inspiration to others as to the triumph we can achieve over seemingly insurmountable odds.

Some of us may be meant for greatness in the larger sense of the word, where public awareness is raised or fame is achieved. Or we may simply be great at what we do. Making cookies for a child's bake sale and having all the cookies sell may make a mother "great" in her child's eyes. Helping a company reach its sales goals by having created a successful ad campaign is an act of "greatness" in the eyes of the company owner.

Know that everything you do matters. Every task, whether large or small, helps fulfill a purpose.

Achieving success on any level should carry with it a sense of happiness, and not just our own. Those who care for us should be happy for our accomplishments, too.

Unfortunately, from time to time jealousy rears its ugly head and even those close to us may react (intentionally or otherwise) in a negative way to our success.

Old friends may no longer be comfortable around us if we are able to afford a luxury car or move to a home in a better neighborhood. Sweet Spirits—if we are able to do these things it is thanks to our hard work and persistence. A true friend should not only realize this but applaud it.

However, if they are unhappy with their own progress in life, they may suddenly find that riding with you in your new car or visiting you in your new home reminds them of what they feel is a "failure" in their own life. Your success may remind them that they have yet to accomplish their own goal.

It is important to tell a jealous friend that you know they can follow and capture their own dreams.

Perhaps they have already achieved something you would like to have achieved. You may have the car and home but wish that you had children like your friend has. Maybe you have an ideal marriage and your friend does not. But perhaps they have a fantastic career they are proud of.

There is something about everyone's life that we may wish we had, and as I have said before, there is nothing wrong with that as long as we do not begrudge their having it. It is not appropriate to want *their* home but it is totally appropriate to desire one *like* it, and then set about finding a way to be able to attract that in your life.

I have always said that "Jealousy is a compliment paid by mediocrity to the genius." Now that may sound harsh at first, but the intent is to explain that someone who is jealous is not an evil person necessarily. They just feel they are inadequate and are looking up to another person with envy, seeing qualities or accomplishments that they may be striving for and wish they had achieved.

Someone else's jealousy is ultimately their problem, not yours. All you can do, if you are aware of the jealousy, is to reassure the person that in no way does your success change the relationship you have with them.

Once we have achieved success, whether business or personal, there is always room for improvement or expansion. So there is never an excuse to give up or stop looking for new horizons to conquer.

I came across an anonymously written quote that sums up the notion of striving for success:

Here is a test to find whether your mission on Earth is finished: if you're alive, it isn't.

7

I love life

In the midst of searching for love, striving for success and making the most of one's moment, it is equally important to take a few precious minutes to rest and recharge our personal batteries, as I have previously mentioned.

To rest, relax and renew is a powerful concept that can do wonders for us mentally, physically, spiritually, and emotionally.

Try to recall how long it has been since you took a break from it all. This does not necessarily mean thinking of when you took a costly or elaborate vacation. Taking a break need not even mean leaving your home. You can sit on your patio and read a book. Do a little gardening if that is what you love to do. Sit quietly and daydream. Reward yourself by watching a movie you have been meaning to see.

Rewarding yourself and taking time for yourself may sound selfish or self-indulgent. "What about my mate, my children, or my pets?" you might ask. Trust me; they will still be there fifteen or twenty minutes later and even two hours later. And they will appreciate the happier, more relaxed person they see.

This does not imply that we should neglect anyone. Rest breaks may need to be timed so as not to interfere with family matters. But it is always possible to find a brief time for peaceful moments alone.

Allow the serenity of this time alone to wash over you. Do not feel guilty. You deserve this time to appreciate life and all it has to offer.

Several years ago I was interviewed by Bruce Fessier, a columnist for Palm Springs' *Desert Sun* newspaper. He met me for tea at what was then the beautiful Givenchy Hotel (it was later purchased by my friend, television star and hotelier, the late Merv Griffin and renamed for Merv).

The owner of the Givenchy was a lovely lady named Rose Narva. She greeted Bruce Fessier and me as we sat down to tea. As I said "hello" to

Rose I heard a spirit voice say, "Tell her that David sends her love." I relayed that message and several others and tears came into her eyes.

"David was my son," she smiled. "He passed away not too long ago."

I told her that he was saying something about "stopping to smell the roses."

She gasped, "That's exactly what he told me so many times. He said my name may be Rose, but did I stop to smell the roses and take time for myself?"

I told her that he hoped she was following that advice now. "I'll show you something," she said. We walked to another area of the hotel and there was an abundant and glorious rose garden.

"I had this garden planted in David's memory, to remind myself to take life easy now and then and to enjoy all that I have. Thank you for the message and please tell David that I'll slow down a little and smell the roses," she said.

The love she had for her beloved son was apparent and I know that he was guiding her and would continue to do so. The love of a mother and child is never broken.

The following is another beautiful story about motherhood.

I was a guest on the Sally Jessy Raphael television show many years ago, and another panel member was the U.K.'s top astrologer, Penny Thornton. Penny had had a successful career as an astrologer when, in 1986, she came to the attention of Diana, Princess of Wales. For the next six years she served as her personal advisor.

Penny and I bonded on the show and have kept in touch ever since. The fact that we had both been advisors to members of the Royal Family was what first caused us to begin a conversation and compare notes about what we felt was in the future for the Royals.

I thought of Penny when writing this book and asked what her moment was. I had expected her to say that it was when she first did the chart of Diana. But while that was undoubtedly one of the great moments of her life, it was a far more personal moment that she chose to relay:

> *By the time you've reached my age, you've almost certainly had more than one life-defining moment, so the challenge was not to find one but to decide which was the one to share. In my case, it wasn't such a difficult task, because I only have to go back to this moment in time to find tears springing to my eyes—not tears of hopelessness or sadness but pure, radiant joy.*

The year was 1982, the date July 9th and the time 05:35 a.m. I mention this because as an astrologer precise moments in time are important.

It was at this exact moment in time that my son, Alexander, was born. It was a moment I had simultaneously longed for and dreaded. You see, he arrived over three months early. When he came into the world, he weighed less than a two-pound bag of sugar and you could hold him in the palm of your hand. He was the tiniest little squawking scrap of humanity.

But to understand why Alexander's birth was such a life-defining event we have to go back even further.

By 1981 I had been a practicing astrologer for some five years. I had already written my first book. I had a thriving astrological practice; I taught, lectured and generally lived astrology. Yet somehow in spite of working with the celestial and the divine I had developed a rather hard-nosed attitude to my fellow man. I had come to believe that we shaped our own destinies. God was an excuse. We blamed too many of our inadequacies, failures and disappointments on factors outside ourselves—the stars being one of them. In fact, I had become a little smug.

As far as my personal life went, I was living happily with my second husband—another astrologer—and my four-year-old son from my first marriage. We had been trying to have a child of our own for a year but I had suffered one miscarriage after another. Yet this was not our only concern. My desire to become pregnant sooner than later was compounded by the fact that the astrological configurations of 1982 looked so dire that we questioned the wisdom of bringing a child into the world at all. However, we decided to press on, making sure that we did not conceive in the months of October and November, which would have meant giving birth in the most difficult month of all, July, 1982.

It did, of course, cross my mind that July's harsh alignments must have some bearing on our lives, since they intersected so perfectly with the family's charts, but, hell, nothing could happen to the baby—he or she wasn't coming into the world until October.

Then, suddenly, inexplicably in May, I went into premature labour. It was all very dramatic. I was shopping in Guildford and, feeling rather woozy, took refuge in the cool of the National West-

minster Bank, whereupon I immediately fainted on the marble floor, sending shopping bags sailing into the lines of curious customers. I was rushed to hospital and found to be four centimeters dilated. Fortunately, I had a courageous and skillful obstetrician, who somehow held back the tide. He performed a Shirodker Suture (a stitch in time and the appropriate place) and attached me to a drip intended to prevent contractions. And there, in Mount Alvernia hospital I remained, committed to total bed rest for weeks on end, a heavy sentence for someone as active as myself. Some five weeks later, it was clear that the baby was not going to wait until October to arrive, so I was moved to London's Queen Charlotte's hospital where they had a superb Special Care Baby unit.

By this time I was already beginning to feel that maybe, just maybe, life wasn't always a case of mind over matter. I mean, I did not want to be in the space I was in. I had definitely not created these events. But here I was, alone in a long, narrow, windowless, soulless room, totally dependent upon other people for my every need. If I dropped so much as a book on the floor, I had to ring for a nurse, who made it clear she had more important things to do. Cut off from my life support systems, I felt disenfranchised, weak and miserable. It was the worst time of my life.

On July 8th, I was moved from my prison of a room to one that was light and airy. My spirits lifted, and, for the first time in weeks, my husband and I spent a happy evening together. We both felt the worst was over. The total lunar eclipse had passed. All would be well. He left at 10 p.m. I went to sleep. At 1:30 a.m., my waters broke. Enter Alexander some four hours later and some thirteen weeks early.

However, the real moment that changed my life was still some hours away.

Once Alex had been born, he was immediately taken to the Special Care Unit and placed in an incubator. We were told he was perfect, but obviously very small, and the next twenty-four hours would be critical. I was wheeled back to my room, exhausted but liberated. And as I lay in my bed, unable to sleep, I came to a decision. I rationalized that there was no point going to see the baby; if he was going to die, which was likely, the less contact I had with his reality, the better. But, somehow this just made me very upset. In fact, every time I thought this thought, I got upset. Finally, just *before lunch, I had an epiphany: if my Alexander lived only for an hour, he was entitled to every bit of love I could give him. In fact, the ferocity of this understanding got me out of my bed and on my spindly legs, careening like a drunk, down the corridor to the nurse's station, demanding to be taken to him.*

I was ten minutes away from the moment that changed my life.

As the sister pushed me in a wheelchair through the doors of Special Care, there was an incubator directly ahead of us. I knew it was Alexander. He was lying on his tummy, a woolly bonnet on his head, and most of the rest of him encased in a disposable diaper. He was not attached to a ventilator, he was breathing on his own, his tiny body moving rapidly up and down with the effort of it all. His face was turned towards me, his little hands outstretched on either side of it, and as I looked at him, slowly and miraculously this huge smile began to appear. He looked me straight in the eye, and smiled at me. A clear and conscious smile of recognition. "Can you see that?" I whispered to the nurse. She nodded, "He is smiling at you; he knows who you are." And there were tears in her eyes, too.

In that instant I was changed. Gone was my understanding that we shaped our destinies, that God was a myth. I knew without a shadow of doubt that I had been given the most profound lesson of my life. I had tried to manipulate the universe by bringing Alexander into the world at a time of my choosing, but despite my best efforts he was born not only in the most difficult month of 1982, but within twenty-four hours of the most difficult day. I had also been given a profound lesson in compassion. During my weeks of incarceration before Alex was born, I discovered what it was like to have no power, to be dependent on others, and to feel weak and frightened. Yet these lessons had been given to me in love. And I had never felt so loved and blessed. From that point on, my life and the way I worked were utterly changed.

There is, of course, a Post Script to this story. Alex came through those perilous early days with flying colours. As one doctor said to us when he was two weeks old, and some half a pound heavier: "It's the will to live that separates the babies who don't make it from those who do. Your Alexander is a fighter—you could leave him overnight on the Hills of Sparta and he'd be there in the morning, screaming with indignation." Our once Alexander the small, is now Alex the great. He owns his own software company and is creating games for I-Phone.

I don't think about his entry into this world every day of my life, but when I do, it not only replenishes my heart but reminds me of my true place in the universal scheme of things. It's a lesson I intend never to repeat.

Today, Penny is author of several books on astrology and has a highly-successful website, Astrolutely.com. But it was the birth of her child and his survival against all odds that stays crystallized in her mind. Love—in any form—truly does make life beautiful.

Just as Penny's moment was a surprise to me, another gentle comment about the beauty of life comes from a surprising source. Russian novelist Fyodor Dostoyevsky often wrote of darkness, struggle and tragedy in such works as *Crime and Punishment, The Brothers Karamazov, The Idiot* and *Notes from the Underground*, but the author's own goodness, light and hope shine through in this personal quote:

Love all God's creation, the whole and every grain of sand in it. Love every leaf, every ray of God's light. Love the animals, love the plants, love everything. If you love everything, you will perceive the divine mystery in things. Once you perceive it, you will begin to comprehend it better every day. And you will come at last to love the whole world with an all-embracing love.

This is a man who truly enjoyed pursuing the simple, gentle side of life, which can often be the most rewarding.

I wrote of my own feelings about living a happy life in a much earlier book, *Guide to Health and Happiness* (Windy Hill Publishing, 1984). I feel it is worth repeating here and is a fine way to conclude this chapter:

I must come first. We must find the peace within ourselves. Be good to yourself. Eat properly, get plenty of rest. You have been given the precious gift of your life so make the most of it. Love yourself and then you can learn to love others.

Live each moment to the fullest. Find new projects; become involved in life.

Offering. Give to your favorite charity. As that donation goes out to help others, you will be justly rewarded. Share part of yourself with others less fortunate.

Vicariously. Aim for the moon. Follow your dreams. Do not live vicariously through other people's lives. Make a wonderful life of your own.

Each day you should pray and meditate. Only Believe; All things are possible if you only believe.

Love those close to you. Let them know you care with more than just words. And as I strongly believe, "I am loyal to my friends and in return I expect my friends to be loyal to me."

Inner voice. Listen to your inner voice and spirit guides. And be grateful for the help you receive.

Fortunate. Be glad to be alive. Every day you wake up you face new and wonderful possibilities.

Eternal. Life is eternal. There are no interruptions. Some say there is only yesterday and today, but no tomorrow. Yet tomorrow is where we will spend the rest of our lives, in this body and in other bodies. We may meet each other with different faces but our souls will be the same.

Like and love one another and you will find inner peace. Start now to pay your karmic debt. This is what "I Love Life" is all about.

My dear friend, talented comic Flip Wilson once sent me a drawing of himself in character as the Reverend Leroy. I share the saying inscribed on the drawing with you: *You may be small in human size, but you're a giant in the Master's eyes.*

8

Our personal moments

When I started writing this book, I knew that I would be asking people from all walks of life, the great and the near-great, to tell me about the moment that changed their life forever.

My co-writer, who has been with me for over thirty years and has co-authored most of my books and hundreds of television shows with me, said, "You will have to tell what moment changed your life, too. I said I would, if she would write about hers, as well.

Ladies first, so here is Valerie's moment:

It's not just because we are writing this book together and not because we've been together more than thirty years, but the moment that changed my life was when I met Kenny Kingston.

Certainly I had enjoyed a happy life before then. I'd enjoyed a wonderful childhood, friends, my high-school and college years. But I knew there was something missing—something I'd yet to attain. I was in my 20s and ready for my life to truly begin.

My interests were the psychic world (something I shared with my father), travel and the entertainment world. I had majored in journalism and radio/tv in college and was eager to start my career.

My friend took me to one of Kenny's spiritualist church meetings. I'd seen him previously on television and felt something special when he came on the screen. I told my friend that I had decided to have a private session with Kenny to sort out my future.

"I feel like I knew him before—in a past life," I told her. I am a strong believer in reincarnation.

"Tell him that when you have your session," she urged. But I knew I wouldn't say anything. It just was not my nature.

I arrived for my appointment a couple of weeks later and sat down at his reading table, given to him by his client Marilyn Monroe. The first thing Kenny said to me was, "We knew each other in a past life."

During the session he brought in, in spirit, my beloved Aunt Nell. He described her perfectly, even to the fact that earrings were important between us. I always gave her earrings or earring-related presents.

He gave me career advice and something just clicked between us that night. We stayed in touch and just began a relationship almost immediately. Kenny likes to say that I came for a reading and never left. It may not have been quite that quick, but it was close.

The life we have led since then has been more than I could have imagined. He's helped bring me out of my shell and he has given me the courage to do and say things I'd never have done or said, because I have known that he believed in me.

I have never had fear of being accepted for my belief in the psychic world because I've been surrounded by Kenny and others who share the belief.

Together, we have traveled to places I had only dreamed of and met people I'd long admired. I have put my writing and radio/television skills to full use with Kenny and have then branched out on my own writing career as well.

If I hadn't met Kenny and my life had taken another path, could I have done some of the things I have done, met some of the people I've met, traveled to some of the places we've gone? Perhaps.

But I have never questioned this or looked back. I have never focused on "what if" or wondered what life would have been like if I hadn't met Kenny, because I feel it was my destiny to have a life with him.

And now, Kenny, it's your turn!

Most people would think my moment would have been when I had my first psychic experience—the first time I encountered a spirit. These episodes were certainly important in the grand scheme of my life. But what I am about to say will have most men reading the pages with their mouths open in disbelief.

What changed my life was the moment I entered the Army. I will never forget the day I was inducted, on May 15. I know some of you may be thinking it was the First World War! But I am happy to clear that up and say it was World War II. I entered the Eighty-eighth Infantry Division of the Army when I was barely eighteen years old.

I was the youngest Army instructor to serve on foreign soil. The United States had lost so many soldiers (non-com's and officers) in combat during the war that we formed the West Point of Europe to train replacement soldiers.

We were located at the Lido Study Center on the Lido de Venezia in Italy, a ten-minute gondola ride from Venice.

The day I left my home in Buffalo, New York, my mother was understandably in tears. But someone of a higher force in the Heavens told me "everything is for the good," so I wasn't worried. I tried to reassure my mother, too.

I had a very good dad and mom—the best. They supported whatever I wanted to do. Until the day my "Greetings…" letter arrived from the U.S. government (there was still a draft at that time), I thought I had my life figured out.

I acknowledged my psychic abilities and welcomed the messages I received, but had yet to see this as my career path. I thought that I wanted to be an actor. At the age of fourteen I joined a local theater stock company in Buffalo and traveled each summer to appear in plays on the East Coast.

Because of this, I was used to spending time away from home. So when the draft letter came from the Army the thought of leaving home did not bother me.

However, I was not a very disciplined young man in the theater, I am sorry to say. Time meant nothing to me. I often liked to nap before the play and overslept often. As an example, I was playing the character of "Arthur" in *The Great Big Doorstep*. The great Louis Calhern was playing my father. The rules were that the company members were to sign in at the theater by 7:45 p.m. for an 8:30 p.m. curtain.

I was in the first scene, barely minutes after the curtain rose. Too many nights, I arrived at the theater as the orchestra was playing *The Star Spangled Banner* (typical in those days). This was just seconds before the curtain rose.

My character was a farm boy with a dirty face. This look should have, of course, been achieved through make-up. But in many cases I dusted my hands on the backstage floor, rubbing them on my face as I heard my cue…and on I went.

So discipline was not a trait that I brought with me to the Army. But I certainly learned it when required to "rise and shine" at a particular time each day and follow a specific routine that a superior officer chose.

The discipline I learned has served me well to this day and is one reason why the Army was my moment. It gave me the stamina, as my post-Army career began, to oftentimes tape two or three television shows in a day or keep a schedule of doing radio shows, private consultations and lecturing that might occupy my time from 9 a.m. till 10:00 p.m.

When we arrived at Fort Dix, New Jersey, for our introduction into the military, we received several very strong inoculation shots. Many of us ran a fever as a result. Several men sat on base holding photos of their wives or girlfriends and crying at their fate. Now there is nothing wrong with this, I suppose. It is quite a sudden lifestyle change.

But I decided then and there to become a survivor. Despite running a fever, I walked to the theater on the base where they were showing films. There were very few of us in attendance.

The film that I saw starred Alexis Smith and Humphrey Bogart, as I recall. I loved it from start to finish. I realized that no matter where I was or how I felt, I could learn to make the best of a situation. My fever broke rather quickly and my outlook was upbeat.

There would be other bases I would be transferred to, including Camp Gordon, Georgia. The discipline lesson I spoke of did not happen overnight, I should mention.

While at Camp Gordon for 16 weeks of basic training, it became unofficially known that I had the dirtiest rifle in camp (I could not be bothered with such an activity as rifle cleaning, I reasoned).

My punishment for this was six weeks of KP—kitchen duty - which I performed after a full day of basic training each day. Truth be told, I loved every minute of it. I had access to food—anything and any time—with no waiting in line.

But it did occur to me that things might not always go as well, so I decided that a little dose of discipline might not be a bad thing to learn.

From Georgia we went to George G. Meade, a base outside of Baltimore, just before being shipped overseas. I recall vicariously tasting spaghetti and knew it was a psychic message that we were being sent to Italy, though the location was meant to be a secret.

When we arrived outside Gorizia, Italy, we were loaded into trucks and taken to the base. It was here that our future in the Army would be decided. If we were not assigned to other posts, we would be sent to active duty in the rifle company.

Famed General Bryant E. Moore was on hand to make the assignments. With our particular group he was looking for a limited number of instructors for the Lido Study Center classes, particularly for courses in military courtesy, public speaking and Army instructional methods. This sounded infinitely better than the rifle company, so I had high hopes of being chosen.

One by one men's names were called and they stated their qualifications. Several men had Master's degrees in English or Education, but General Moore would say, "Fall out," meaning their fate in the rifle company was sealed.

I thought quickly and when my name was called, I said, "Sir, I've appeared in eight Broadway plays," and I held my breath.

"Excellent! Excellent!" General Moore said, and I was on my way to becoming an instructor.

Now technically, I had not appeared in the plays *on* Broadway. I had appeared in local stock companies that were offering plays that had been *done on Broadway*. But needless to say, I had not mentioned this and the General chose to believe what he wanted. The truth is, my time in the theater no doubt did serve me well when teaching public speaking and related courses.

During my time on the Lido I had the pleasure of meeting many distinguished people and becoming at ease around them and this was another momentous lesson. Tobacco heiress Doris Duke was in Italy as a "reporter" (though I am not sure how much reporting she actually did, but it was a way for her to travel to Italy). I met her when she looked in on one of my classes one day, and we struck up a friendship.

I met and gave a reading to violin virtuoso Yehudhi Menuhin, who was entertaining the troops. My psychic abilities could not be silenced even during my Army days. I gave messages to General Dwight David Eisenhower and met Italian actresses Alida Valli and Valentina Cortese. They became my friends after I gave them psychic messages.

While strolling the beach one day, I met American party giver extraordinaire Elsa Maxwell, who was staying at the villa of Britain's Duke and Duchess of Windsor. She introduced me to them and that began my association with them as their psychic.

I also met American actor Dan Dailey, who was serving in Special Services. We became friends and I assisted him with projects, booking shows for the Allied Theatre.

During this time, opera singer Grace Moore was booked to play Venice's La Fenice Opera House and Dan had been asked to introduce her. For some reason (probably because even though he was a song-and-dance man, he knew nothing and cared nothing about the opera), Dan said he did not want to do it and asked me to do the honors, which I, of course, did.

Grace was apparently pleased with my abilities as an announcer and asked for me to be her announcer as she traveled to various bases in Italy, giving concerts. By then our school had closed and I had joined Special Services full time because Dan was leaving.

My skills as an announcer and Master of Ceremonies emerged as I traveled with Grace. This is another reason the Army was my moment. I learned stage presence and entertainment techniques that I believe have set me apart from other psychics.

My military obligation was quickly coming to an end and my superior officer asked me to stay on in my current position. He even offered me an advancement. I gave it serious thought, but had come to the conclusion that my psychic abilities were only growing stronger and I longed to use them while also entertaining people. So I declined the offer.

Grace requested that I join her for one last segment of her military tour. This would be a concert in Copenhagen and then in Sweden. I was flattered, but told her I was leaving the military and my days as an announcer were behind me. She was very persuasive and said she would leave the offer open until the very last minute. I nearly reconsidered.

But in the end I stayed firm in my decision. "Well, then, I wish you all the best," she said. "Please promise me that you'll meet my dear friends Clifton Webb and his mother Mabelle when you return to New York. They've been leasing my townhouse," she said. She told me that Clifton was appearing at the Plymouth Theatre in Noel Coward's *Present Laughter* and that I should see him in the production and then go backstage and tell him I was a friend of hers.

I was given leave at Christmastime and went home. It was at this point that my life was actually saved because of my decision. Though I had yet to be officially discharged from the Army (that would come in February), I was allowed to go home. My time had been served.

I followed Grace's suggestion and went to see Clifton. This was the beginning of a longtime friendship for me with Clifton and his mother. As many people know, when Clifton passed, he became one of my spirit guides and often provides humorous touches during my nightclub and lecture appearances. I have Grace to thank for the friendship.

One night in January I was listening to my radio in New York. I had dozed off but woke up to the tail end of a news story that I believed announced a place crash involving Grace Moore and Prince Gustav Adolf of Sweden.

I immediately called Grace's townhouse and Mabelle Webb answered. "No, dear, I'm sure you're wrong," she said soothingly. "Everything's fine with Grace. You were probably half asleep."

But I continued listening to the radio and Mabelle called me a few minutes later. By then we had both heard the story and knew it was true. Grace's plane had crashed as it took off for Sweden from Copenhagen. All aboard had perished, including Grace and the Prince of Sweden, who was traveling with her back to his homeland.

But for the grace of God, and because my spirit impulses had told me to leave my post as her announcer, I would have perished with her. There had been one seat vacant next to Grace which had not been filled. It was intended to be MINE.

Losing a dear friend and knowing my life had been spared, I pressed on with pursuing my career as a psychic and have never regretted it for even one second. It has given me enormous satisfaction to help countless people, and I have continued to travel and meet many wonderful friends from all walks of life, but particularly from the social, entertainment and political worlds.

The late Dominick Dunne will always hold a soft spot in my heart because he was often accused of name-dropping. I have been told the same thing on one or two occasions.

But neither of us could help telling the stories we told. These are the people we have known and the circles we have traveled in.

And so, inspired by Dominick, I set out now to write my autobiography. It will be called *I've Known Them All from A to Z*.

Index

9/11	35	Eisenhower, Dwight David	101
		Emerson, Ralph Waldo	79
Alda, Alan	50		
Ambassador Hotel	77	Fessier, Bruce	89
Apports	14	Fine, Gretchen	23-24, 45
Astaire, Fred	76-77	Free will	14
Auras	36-37	*From Here to Eternity*	26
Bacon, James	25-26		
Barnes, Billy	21	Garland, Beverly	6-7, 86
Bible reference	14	Givenchy Hotel	89
Brown, David	30	Goals	67
Brown, Helen Gurley	29-30	Gorme, Eydie	75-76
Burghoff, Gary	50	Gratitude	15, 19
		Griffin, Merv	89
Caldwell, Taylor	65		
Charles, Prince	37	Haber, Mel	48, 72-73
Cosmopolitan Magazine	29, 30	Hauser, Gayelord	47
Cornell, Katharine	57-58	Hope, Bob	49, 82-83
Crosby, Bing	7	Hopper, Hedda	29
		Hughes, Howard	79-80
Dailey, Dan	101, 102		
Death	62, 63-65	Hutton, Betty	12-13
deSalles, St. Frances	56		
Diana, Princess	36-37, 90	"If only"	38-40
		Ingleside Inn	72
Diller, Phyllis	49, 82-84, 85, 86		
Dishell, Dr. Walter	50, 63, 84-85	Keller, Helen	86
Divine Order	11	Kenwith, Herbert	68
Dostoyevsky, Fyodor	94	Kingston, mom Kaye	23, 25, 47
Dunne, Dominick	40-42, 103	Kingston, Kenny	43, 44, 45, 46, 47, 48, 49, 51, 52, 97-103
Dunne, Dominique	40-42		
		Kingston, Kenny web site	37

Jackson, Michael	7	Saying yes	33-34
Jorgensen, Christine	23-24, 45	*Sex & the Single Girl*	30
		Sex reassignment surgery	23
Lawrence, Steve	48, 75-76	*Sextette*	68
Lee, Michele	56-57, 58	Simon, Sam	21-22
Lover, Vagabond	7-8	*Simpsons, The*	21-22
		Sinatra, Frank	7, 25-26
MacArthur, Gen. Douglas	16	Smith, Robyn	77
Marshall, Garry	49, 81	Spirit world	62-63
		Stage mothers	24
M*A*S*H	50, 85	Staunton, Imelda	36
Maugham, W. Somerset	69	Struthers, Sally	46, 61-62
Maxwell, Elsa	101	Sub-moments	16
Melvyn's Restaurant	48	Suicide	37-38
Menuhin, Yehudi	52, 101	Sullivan, Susan	49, 81-82
Mini vacation	58-59, 89	Swit, Loretta	50
Moore, Gen. Bryant E.	101		
Moore, Grace	102-103	Teresa, Mother	73-74
Morton, Andrew	37	Thornton, Penny	50, 90-94
		Truman, Bess Wallace	5, 86
Need vs. want	9-11	Truman, President Harry	5, 9, 16, 86
New Year's Day	69	Truman, Margaret	6
Newley, Anthony	1, 43		
		Vallee, Eleanor	7-8, 43
Omens	14	Vallee, Rudy	7-8, 43
Once in a Lifetime	1	*Vanity Fair Magazine*	40
		Vera Drake	36
Peace of mind	19-20	Victim, being	70-72
Philbin, Regis	23, 68		
Porter, Valerie	9, 49, 59-60, 97	Webb, Clifton	102
Presley, Elvis	7	Webber, Andrew Lloyd	55
Psychic hotline infomercial	33-34	West, Mae	47, 67-68
		"What if"	38-40
Raphael, Sally Jessy	90	Wilson, Flip	51, 96
Reynolds, Debbie	11-13, 44	Windsor, Duke &	
Rice, Tim	55	Duchess of	84-85, 101
		Worley, Jo Anne	20-21, 44
		Wright, Cobina	47